THEOLOGY, POLITICS,
AND EXEGESIS

THEOLOGY, POLITICS, AND EXEGESIS

Essays on the History
of Modern Biblical Criticism

Jeffrey L. Morrow

To Nick and Carol,
My biggest fans! In
Thanks and with much love,
and so many fond memories from
my youth,

Jeffry L. Morrow

PICKWICK *Publications* · Eugene, Oregon

THEOLOGY, POLITICS, AND EXEGESIS
Essays on the History of Modern Biblical Criticism

Pickwick Publications
An Imprint of Wipf and Stock Publishers
199 W. 8th Ave., Suite 3
Eugene, OR 97401

www.wipfandstock.com

PAPERBACK ISBN: 978-1-5326-1492-7
HARDCOVER ISBN: 978-1-5326-1494-1
EBOOK ISBN: 978-1-5326-1493-4

Cataloging-in-Publication data:

Names: Morrow, Jeffrey L.
Title: Theology, politics, and exegesis : essays on the history of modern biblical criticism / Jeffrey L. Morrow.
Description: Eugene, OR : Imprint, 2017 | Includes bibliographical references and index.
Identifiers: ISBN 978-1-5326-1492-7 (paperback) | ISBN 978-1-5326-1494-1 (hardcover) | ISBN 978-1-5326-1493-4 (ebook)
Subjects: LCSH: Biblical Hermeneutics. | Bible—Criticism, interpretation, etc.—History—Modern period, 1500–.
Classification: LCC BS500 M76 2017 (print) | LCC BS500 (ebook)

Manufactured in the U.S.A.   10/05/17

This book is dedicated to Scott W. Hahn, William L. Portier, Edwin M. Yamauchi, and James C. Hanges, in thanksgiving for their friendship and mentorship over the years, especially while I was a student.

CONTENTS

ACKNOWLEDGMENTS

MUCH OF THE MATERIAL in this book began as conference presentations, book review essays, and scholarly articles that are here collected, revised, and presented as a unified volume. The first chapter began as a review essay of Scott Hahn's and Benjamin Wiker's 2013 volume *Politicizing the Bible: The Roots of Historical Criticism and the Secularization of Scripture 1300–1700*. The review was published as "The Untold History of Modern Biblical Scholarship's Pre-Enlightenment Secular Origins," *Journal of Theological Interpretation* 8.1 (2014) 145–55. In its present form it is greatly revised and expanded, and is here reused with permission, for which I thank the *Journal of Theological Interpretation*.

The second chapter began as a scholarly paper I presented at the annual meeting of the Society of Biblical Literature in San Diego, California, on November 24, 2014, in the History of Interpretation Unit. That paper was entitled, "The Natural and Supernatural, Ceremony and the Heart: Spinoza's Use of the Psalms." I later revised that paper and expanded it, and that new version was published as "Spinoza's Use of the Psalms in the Context of His Political Project," *Interdisciplinary Journal of Research on Religion* 11 (2015) 1–18. This article is here revised yet again, and is used with permission, for which I thank the *Interdisciplinary Journal of Research on Religion*.

The third chapter began as a research project for a paper Matthew Levering invited me to present, but for which I had to back out early, after much research was completed, but prior to having written any paper, because of the expected birth of our third child, Patrick. I thank Matthew for the invitation and providing me a reason to work with the writings of Richard Simon and St. Thomas More. This chapter represents the second half of the later paper I eventually produced, the first half of which is forthcoming as "The Acid of History: La Peyrère, Hobbes, Spinoza, and the Separation of Faith and Reason in Modern Biblical Studies," *Heythrop Journal*. The second part, on which this third chapter is based, was published as "Faith, Reason and History in Early Modern Catholic Biblical Interpretation: Fr. Richard Simon and St. Thomas More," *New Blackfriars* 96 (2015) 658–73. It is here revised, and I thank *New Blackfriars* for permission to reuse it.

The fourth chapter began as a very lengthy review essay of Michael Legaspi's 2010 *The Death of Scripture and the Rise of Biblical Studies*, which grew out of his 2006 Harvard University doctoral dissertation. Matthew Levering solicited the review essay initially as a much shorter review, for *Nova et Vetera*. I had already read Legaspi's very important unpublished dissertation, and was excited to read the published version which Oxford University Press published. Not long into it, I recognized its importance, and the ways in which it improved upon the unpublished version, and so I asked Matthew for permission to transform the short review into a much longer essay. I thank Matthew and his then co-editor, Reinhard Hütter, for publishing such a lengthy review essay, which turned into a sort of survey of the history of scholarship on the history of modern biblical criticism. That essay was originally published as "The Enlightenment University and the Creation of the Academic Bible: Michael Legaspi's *The Death of Scripture and the Rise of Biblical Studies*," *Nova et Vetera* 11.3 (2013) 897–922. I have greatly revised that review essay, and I thank *Nova et Vetera*, and the St. Paul Center for Biblical Theology, which now publishes *Nova et Vetera*, for granting me permission to reuse this material.

Finally, the fifth chapter began as a scholarly paper I presented at The Second International Conference of Catholic Theological Ethics in the World Church, in Trent, Italy, as part of their Research and Reconciliation Panel, on July 25, 2010. That paper was entitled, "The Political Background to the Separation of the Bible from Theological Ethics prior to Vatican II." I owe a word of thanks to Maria Morrow and Biff Rocha for critiquing earlier drafts of that initial paper, and I also owe thanks to Scott Hahn and Benjamin Wiker for providing me with early drafts of their *Politicizing the Bible* manuscript prior to publication for this paper, as well for many fruitful conversations, with both Scott and Ben, that helped me in that initial paper.

I also owe Fr. James Keenan, S.J. a tremendous word of thanks for his warm welcome of my wife and me at Trent; he generously made our travel and stay there possible with a grant for younger scholars. Fr. Jim facilitated a truly international conference where we had the pleasure of getting to know so many moral theologians from across the globe, including many from South America, Africa, and Asia. It was a wonderful sharing of ideas. I feel especially grateful that he accepted my paper, when I am more of an outsider to moral theology. I benefitted greatly from the discussion after my presentation. We travelled there with our second child, our daughter, Eva, and had a wonderful experience in Venice and Padua on our way to Trent. I also owe Immaculate Conception Seminary School of Theology at Seton Hall University, and the Seminary's Rector and Dean, who at that time was Msgr. Robert Coleman, a word of thanks for helping defray the costs involved in my travelling to Trent to present that paper.

This paper continued to evolve and expand as I continued to work on it in light of feedback I was receiving. I later published a greatly expanded version of this paper as "Cut Off from Its Wellspring: The Politics Behind the Divorce of Scripture from Catholic Moral Theology," *Heythrop Journal* 56.4 (2015) 547–58. I owe my wife Maria Morrow, and also Biff Rocha, thanks again for critiquing a number of drafts of this article after the Trent conference. Thanks are due as well to *Heythrop Journal* for permission to reuse this article, which is here revised. Unless otherwise mentioned, all English translations throughout this volume are my own. Kathryn Feilmeyer read the entire volume and corrected numerous typos and errors, for which I am greatly indebted. All infelicities remain my own.

I have dedicated this work to four of the most significant mentors I had throughout my undergraduate and graduate education: Scott W. Hahn, William L. Portier, Edwin M. Yamauchi, and James C. Hanges. Scott Hahn, whose work served as the topic of my doctoral dissertation, has become a good friend over the years. I continue to treasure his friendship, guidance, assistance, prayers, and advice. He remains one of my most important spiritual benefactors. Bill Portier was my doctoral advisor, but he was much more than a dissertation director; he was a true mentor. I learned as much about life from him as I did about the topics I studied with him during the four doctoral seminars I took from him, dissertation work, and exam preparation. I have many fond memories from our time spent at Tanks, Milano's, and other sundry locations. I spent many hours in the office of Edwin Yamauchi, "Dr. Y," as an undergraduate. He always made time for me, even before I ever took any of his classes. His work was important in my initial conversion to Christianity, when I self-identified as a Jewish agnostic, and he modeled for me what it meant to be a Christian scholar. I took more undergraduate courses and directed studies from Jim Hanges, something close to twenty credit hours, than from any other professor, and I spent almost as much time in his office hours or up town at Mac and Joe's or Skipper's as I did in class. I learned more about how to conduct research from him than from anyone else, and I learned a lot from our intellectual sparring sessions.

INTRODUCTION

IN THREE SKEPTICS AND *the Bible*, I provided an overview of the history of modern biblical criticism from late antiquity to the nineteenth century.[1] The majority of the book, however, focused on the seventeenth century works of Isaac La Peyrère (c. 1596 to 1676),[2] Thomas Hobbes (1588 to 1679),[3] and Baruch Spinoza (1632 to 1677).[4] I concluded that work with a look at an important shift that occurred in the modern period. Scripture went from being viewed as a living work made for the sacred liturgy and instead became viewed as a book, like any other. I focused especially on the role of Hobbes and Spinoza and the related redefinition of the term "religion" during this time period.[5] That volume originated from prior work I had published in other less accessible venues, built upon research I had been engaged in since 2005 while still a doctoral student.[6]

In some ways, this present volume serves as a sequel to *Three Skeptics*. It too is derived from earlier work I have done, and stems from my desire to explore the history of modern biblical criticism, getting at its roots, uncovering its often hidden philosophical and political influences, examining its limits, and searching for a means of integrating traditional theological inquiry with biblical exegesis.[7] I begin this volume with a

1. Morrow, *Three Skeptics and the Bible*, 10–53.

2. Ibid., 54–84.

3. Ibid., 85–103.

4. Ibid., 104–38.

5. Ibid., 139–49.

6. Specifically, they derived from Morrow, "Politics of Biblical Interpretation," 528–45; Morrow, "Modernist Crisis," 265–80; Morrow, "French Apocalyptic Messianism," 203–13; Morrow, "Pre-Adamites," 1–25; Morrow, "*Leviathan*," 33–54; Morrow, "Historical Criticism," 189–221; and Morrow, "Bible in Captivity," 285–99.

7. The prior works referred to here are Morrow, "Untold History," 145–55; Morrow, "Spinoza's Use of the Psalms," 1–18; Morrow, "Faith, Reason and History," 658–73;

briefer and less broad overview of the political and philosophical history of the late medieval and early modern roots of historical criticism, and then I move through the seventeenth and eighteenth centuries focusing on three cases in point. I conclude with a look at the separation of Catholic moral theology from biblical studies in the twentieth century.

In chapter 1, taking Scott Hahn and Benjamin Wiker as my guide, I plow through the political and philosophical history behind the advent of modern biblical criticism roughly from 1300 to 1700.[8] Following the outline of their important volume, *Politicizing the Bible*, I begin with a look at Marsilius of Padua (1275 to 1342) and William of Ockham (1285 to 1347), underscoring the context of the conflict between Pope John XXII and Ludwig of Bavaria, as well as the Latin Averroist tradition, for understanding their work pertaining to Scriptural interpretation.[9] I then discuss the importance of John Wycliffe (1320 to 1384) and the ways in which he unwittingly and unintentionally carried forward the Ockhamite exegetical project.[10] Next we encounter Niccolò Machiavelli (1469 to 1527) and his initiation of a hermeneutic of suspicion.[11]

After Machiavelli, we come to the Protestant Reformation and the towering figure of Martin Luther (1483 to 1546) and the many ways in which his challenges to tradition inadvertently prepared for what would come in the far more skeptical side of modern biblical criticism.[12] After Luther comes King Henry VIII and the various political doings of the English Reformation which, grounded in the thought of both Machiavelli and Wycliffe, prepared English soil for later Deistic biblical criticism which would eventually transplant to Germany and influence the shape of modern biblical criticism for centuries to come.[13] The last stage of the philosophical, historical, and methodological groundwork is set by a brief discussion of René Descartes (1596 to 1650) and his cosmological transformation mechanizing nature and pushing the question of method to the forefront.[14]

Morrow, "Enlightenment University," 897–922; and Morrow, "Cut Off from Its Wellspring," 547–58.

8. Hahn and Wiker, *Politicizing the Bible*. More recently, see also my more lengthy review of their work, Morrow, "Averroism, Nominalism, and Mechanization," 1293–1340.

9. See Hahn and Wiker, *Politicizing the Bible*, 23–57.

10. See ibid., 61–115.

11. See ibid., 117–46.

12. See ibid., 147–219.

13. See ibid., 221–55.

14. See ibid., 257–84.

After the brief history of this methodological groundwork is discussed, we turn to Hobbes, whom I discussed in more detail in *Three Skeptics*.[15] Hobbes contributes to Scripture's evisceration through his explicitly political exegesis. Next comes Spinoza, who had been another focus of *Three Skeptics* and whose philosophical *Tractatus theologico–politicus* laid the methodological foundation in his seventh chapter for a scientific exegesis which would form the basis of modern biblical criticism.[16] Then comes Richard Simon (1638 to 1712), who had been a close friend of La Peyrère, and to whom chapter 3 of this present volume is dedicated.[17] Simon's context in King Louis XIV's seventeenth-century France forces his exegetical work to take on a certain ambiguity, but a careful reading shows the ways in which he continued the work of his earlier contemporaries, La Peyrère, Hobbes, and Spinoza. After Simon comes John Locke (1632 to 1704), whose work, forged in the political intrigue of the English Civil Wars, built upon prior biblical hermeneutics (especially that of Simon) and took them further.[18] Finally, I bring this initial chapter to a close with some comments about the Deist John Toland (1670 to 1722), who furthered the skeptical projects of Spinoza et al., and influenced eighteenth-century German biblical criticism via Johann Salomo Semler (1725 to 1791) et al.[19]

In chapter 2 we return to Spinoza for a more specific investigation into his exegesis. In *Three Skeptics*, I situated Spinoza in the context of the politics of the Dutch Republic in the seventeenth century, looking in depth at the variety of intellectual influences on his thought, as well as looking at the specifics of his proposed methodological program for biblical criticism. In this chapter I look at the way he uses the biblical Psalms in his *Tractatus theologico-politicus*, examining each instance of his citing, quoting, or alluding to the Psalms in that foundational work. I show how his use of the Psalms fits within his overall political project.

In chapter 3, I turn to the work of Richard Simon and St. Thomas More (1478 to 1535). The exclusion of Simon from *Three Skeptics* was a glaring oversight, since Simon's seventeenth century work was in some ways more important, and certainly more modern and critical, than that of La Peyrère, Hobbes, or Spinoza. Often, especially in the world of

15. See Morrow, *Three Skeptics and the Bible*, 85–103; and Hahn and Wiker, *Politicizing the Bible*, 258–338.

16. See Morrow, *Three Skeptics and the Bible*, 104–38; and Hahn and Wiker, *Politicizing the Bible*, 339–93.

17. See Hahn and Wiker, *Politicizing the Bible*, 395–423.

18. See ibid., 425–86.

19. See ibid., 487–541.

Catholic biblical scholarship, Richard Simon is touted as a helpful seventeenth century response to Spinoza's destructive biblical hermeneutic. Those scholars who recognize the problems with Spinoza's more skeptical approach, but want to salvage his proposed scientific biblical method, look at Simon, Catholic priest and scholar, as an example of faithfully using modern historical biblical criticism from a position of faith so as to enrich theology. This is possible because of the way Simon fashions his historical critical work as a response to the more skeptical exegesis of Hobbes and Spinoza. Simon also attempted to defend Catholic tradition to his Calvinist interlocutors.

Upon closer inspection, however, I argue that Simon's work merely took Spinoza's method further, multiplying the apparent difficulties of Scripture. If we seek to look for an earlier example of a faithful integration of faith and reason, theology and history, from the modern period, I suggest the work of St. Thomas More. More argued for the importance of textual criticism, philology, and history, and yet he understood the necessity of traditional modes of exegesis as well, all under the guidance of the Magisterium, so that biblical interpretation could proceed from the heart of the church.

Chapter 4 takes this history further into the eighteenth century. Following the important work of Michael Legaspi, I look at the figure of Johann David Michaelis (1717 to 1791) at the University of Göttingen in historical context.[20] After a brief overview of the history of the relatively recent discipline of the history of biblical scholarship, I discuss the rise of the Enlightenment university and its place in the culture and history of Germany.[21] I then walk through the transformation of classical studies at the University of Göttingen under Michaelis's senior and friend Johann Matthias Gesner (1691 to 1761) and Gesner's successor, Christian Gottlob Heyne (1729 to 1812).[22] Next I explore Michaelis's place as a Hebrew philologist and his transformation of biblical studies into an autonomous academic discipline within the Enlightenment university, ensuring its survival.[23] Then I look at the influence of English criticism and specifically Robert Lowth (1710 to 1787) on Michaelis and Michaelis's mediation of Lowth's work in Germany.[24] I conclude this chapter with an examination

20. See Legaspi, *Death of Scripture*.

21. See ibid., 27–51.

22. See ibid., 53–78.

23. See ibid., 79–104.

24. See ibid., 105–28.

of the role of Moses and the Mosaic question in the context of Michaelis's work.[25]

I conclude this volume with chapter 5 where I look at the separation of biblical studies from Catholic moral theology. The role of Scripture in moral theology is, in general, a much neglected study.[26] In many ways, this builds on the history already discussed. The eighteenth-century focus on *Wissenschaft*, scholarship, like that epitomized by the scholars like Michaelis at the University of Göttingen, led to the increasing specialization in pre-theological areas of study, like Northwest Semitic philology, archaeology, and Assyriology. The modernist crisis at the dawn of the twentieth century, with roots in the end of the nineteenth century, marked the entrance of modern biblical criticism in the Catholic world. Scholars like Alfred Loisy (1857 to 1940) engaged in such methods and eventually got in trouble with the Magisterium of the Church. Loisy was excommunicated in 1908, the year after Pope St. Pius X's famous condemnation of modernism as the "synthesis of all heresies" in his *Pascendi Dominici Gregis*.

My hope in this volume is to make my work on these related areas within the history of modern biblical scholarship available to a broader audience. This volume represents my continued attempts to provide the sort of "criticism of criticism" that Pope Emeritus Benedict XVI called for in his "Biblical Interpretation in Conflict."[27] As we continue to examine the roots of modern biblical criticism, its philosophical and political underpinnings, as well as benefits and limits, will become more apparent. Hopefully, we will better be able to work towards a more faithful integration of theology and exegesis.

25. See ibid., 129–53.

26. Exceptions include Siker, *Scripture in Ethics*.

27. Ratzinger, *Schriftsauslegung im Widerstreit*.

1

AN OVERVIEW OF THE HISTORY OF BIBLICAL CRITICISM PRIOR TO THE ENLIGHTENMENT

IN THIS FIRST CHAPTER, I provide a brief overview of the history of biblical criticism prior to the eighteenth century. The chapter will be much briefer than the first chapter in my earlier *Three Skeptics and the Bible*, and it will not cover as broad a terrain, but it will help orient readers to prepare for the subsequent chapters in this volume. Here I follow the basic outline of Scott Hahn and Benjamin Wiker's *Politicizing the Bible: The Roots of Historical Criticism and the Secularization of Scripture 1300–1700*.[1] I rely on their work for the most part because it remains the most important work to date in the history of modern biblical scholarship. They show the ways in which the interpretation and the study of Scripture have been secularized over the course of centuries, sometimes inadvertently, but often for the express purpose of being redeployed as a political tool. The role of politics and philosophy has been addressed only rarely or briefly in surveys of biblical scholarship. Filling in that gap was one of the main purposes of my prior work, *Three Skeptics and the Bible*. I continue that work in this volume.

Hahn and Wiker's more thorough treatment in *Politicizing the Bible* lucidly and eruditely demonstrates how various political concerns and

---

1. This chapter originated as a lengthy book review of their volume in Morrow, "Untold History," 145–55.

1

undergirding philosophies shaped and guided the long process which led to the historical-critical method of biblical interpretation. They situate this process within historical, political, philosophical, and theological contexts, and through the biographies of the key figures, which prove so necessary for understanding this history. Moreover, they consider an expansive and often neglected period within the history of modern biblical criticism—namely, the fourteenth through seventeenth centuries. In this present volume, I take that history further, delving into the eighteenth, nineteenth, and even twentieth centuries.

I am in agreement with Hahn and Wiker's overarching argument, articulated in their first chapter, "that the development of the historical–critical method in biblical studies is only fully intelligible as part of the more comprehensive project of secularization that occurred in the West over the last seven hundred years, and that the politicizing of the Bible was, in one way or another, essential to this project."[2] Hahn and Wiker's work demonstrates that the historical-critical method has far deeper roots than is generally considered. Whereas scholars are accustomed to dating the historical-critical method of biblical studies to the nineteenth century, or perhaps the eighteenth century, they extend the genealogical tree back into the fourteenth century. The figures they examine, moreover, indicate the link between the roots of historical-criticism and modern politics. As we examine this history, what we discover is that the distinctiveness of modern historical biblical criticism is not the various scholarly tools of textual criticism, philology, archaeology, etc., but rather, "This union of tools with secularizing presuppositions."[3]

Marsilius of Padua and William of Ockham

Although, as I showed in *Three Skeptics and the Bible*,[4] the roots of historical-criticism are even deeper than Hahn and Wiker's volume would at first appear to indicate, we can pick up the story where they begin

---

2. Hahn and Wiker, *Politicizing the Bible*, 8. Throughout this chapter, I will be borrowing freely from Hahn's and Wiker's work, citing specific pages where important. Unless otherwise mentioned, assume the main material is coming from their helpful chapters.

3. Ibid., 12.

4. Morrow, *Three Skeptics and the Bible*, 12–15 and 60–64. Because of the topic, and the heavy reliance on Hahn's and Wiker's work, there will be some overlap here with my more thorough treatment in ibid., 10–53.

with Marsilius of Padua (1275 to 1342)[5] and William of Ockham (1285 to 1347),[6] both of whom argued for the subordination of the church to the state, through Averroist and nominalist philosophies respectively. The proximate context of these two figures is the Avignon Papacy and the Franciscan poverty debate,[7] both of which are essential for understanding the historical and political background to their discussions of Scripture. This debate involved not only Pope John XXII (reigned from 1316 to 1334), but also Ludwig of Bavaria, who used the Franciscan poverty issue as a political means of attacking the papacy.[8]

Marsilius and Ockham found themselves right in the middle of these controversies, as they both came to reside under Ludwig's protection from John XXII. The Latin Averroism of Marsilius entailed the "superiority of the truths of natural reason to those of revelation."[9] An important work in this context is Marsilius's political treatise *Defensor Pacis*, an anti–papal text which Marsilius completed in 1324. The politics of Marsilius's work were grounded in reason apart from faith with the primary practical concern of securing civil peace, which he regarded as the highest good. Marsilius used Scripture whenever he was able to twist its interpretation to serve merely secular ends. In the end, the secular state Marsilius envisioned was to be in control of biblical interpretation as well as church offices so that the state could control ecclesiastical decisions.[10]

Ockham would eventually join Marsilius, but with a different and more spiritual purpose. Ockham got into trouble with John XXII, and fled Avignon to the protection of Ludwig. From the safety of Ludwig's protection, Ockham attacked the papacy while seeking to reinstate the medieval view of sacred and secular as two distinct powers.[11] Because Ockham saw an extraordinary need for church reform, he argued for the ability and necessity of secular rulers to rule over sinful prelates. Related to this was Ockham's emphasis on the role of biblical specialists who should be in charge of biblical interpretation.[12]

---

5. Hahn and Wiker, *Politicizing the Bible*, 23–39.

6. Ibid., 39–57.

7. Ibid., 18–22.

8. Ibid.

9. Ibid., 23.

10. Ibid., 24–34.

11. Ibid., 40. On the complexity involved in the medieval social order, see especially Jones, *Before Church and State*.

12. Hahn and Wiker, *Politicizing the Bible*, 44–47.

John Wycliff

After this Marsilius and Ockham, John Wycliff (1320 to 1384) emerges as an important but too often neglected figure within this history.[13] Wycliffe's attack upon nominalism inadvertently supported the same sort of exegesis and subordination of the church to the state as had Marsilius and Ockham evidenced prior to Wycliffe. Thus, for theological reasons (and philosophical reasons directly opposed to Ockham) Wycliffe brought to English and, through his followers, to German soil the subordination of church to state for which Marsilius had argued for secular reasons, and which Ockham had argued for related theological reasons. Thus, the ground was set for the German and English Reformations which would soon follow. Wycliffe's metaphysical realism grounded his entire theo-political exegetical project. Wycliffe passionately argued that the state had an obligation to control the civil realm and should thus take control of the church's temporal goods.[14]

Niccolò Machiavelli

Niccolò Machiavelli (1469 to 1527) is another important but too often neglected figure within this history.[15] Machiavelli created a hermeneutic of suspicion, where, much like Averroës (but influenced in fact by Greek historians like Polybius and Plutarch), Machiavelli saw religion as a veil for more crafty political machinations of hypocritical rulers. Though he is not renowned as a biblical interpreter, Machiavelli's social and historical context in Florence of the latter-half of the fifteenth century is essential to understanding his oeuvre, and thus his contribution to the later development of historical criticism. The universally recognized instances of the corruption of the papacy and of some members of the clergy constitute the necessary background to this social and historical context. Hahn and Wiker observe that, "in view of the notorious doings of the papacy and Church hierarchy during this period, religious hypocrisy had gone from being a scandal to an art. The damage done to the faith of the Church by the popes during Machiavelli's lifetime is incalculable."[16]

---

13. In addition to ibid., 61–115 on Wycliffe, see also Levy, *Holy Scripture and the Quest for Authority*, 54–91.

14. Hahn and Wiker, *Politicizing the Bible*, 66.

15. Ibid., 117–46.

16. Ibid., 118.

In *The Prince*, Machiavelli seeks to effect a transformation of politics from its ancient otherworldly orientation to a wholly this-worldly focus where the "goal is the preservation of power."[17] Machiavelli sought to secularize all politics for the very Marsilian goal of terrestrial peace, and in so doing he effected "a fundamental shift in the treatment of Scripture."[18] The biblical Moses was placed in the context of pagan political leaders, effectively secularizing his role within Scripture and making him "a merely political leader," rather than one called by God to mediate God's covenant with the Israelites.[19] Machiavelli was convinced that the biblical account needed such a "corrective" to make the Bible's history read more like Plutarch's. With his *Discourses on Livy*, Machiavelli was consciously trying to create a modern critical history, where he could recover history "shorn of the Christian overlay and interpretation."[20] Within this account, Machiavelli shifted the question from religious veracity to political utility.[21] Hahn and Wiker describe Machiavelli as "one of the earliest, and certainly the most influential, sources of the hermeneutics of suspicion."[22]

Martin Luther

After Machiavelli, the Protestant Reformers emerge as important transitional sixteenth century figures within this history. Looking at Martin Luther (1483 to 1546) we can see the many ways he inadvertently contributed to what would eventually become historical-criticism.[23] Luther was a nominalist, a self-identified follower of Ockham, who shared in the criticism of ecclesiastical corruption and built upon the groundwork laid by Marsilius and Wycliffe, inadvertently aiding in the transformation of the public civic realm into a secular realm, wherein the state controlled the church.

Luther cannot be fully understood without being situated in his broader nominalist context.[24] This is one of the main insights Heiko Oberman's work, and that of his academic disciples, has contributed to

17. Ibid., 128.
18. Ibid., 131.
19. Ibid.
20. Ibid., 138.
21. Ibid., 140.
22. Ibid., 144.
23. Ibid., 147–219.
24. Ibid., 147–50.

Reformation histories.[25] Another essential context for understanding the Reformation, including changes in biblical exegesis, is the political context.[26] The political context provides the necessary lens for understanding the rest of the history of Luther's work, but also of the Reformation more broadly, and all of the various political contexts to the theological and exegetical moves Luther and his other contemporaries make.[27]

Luther's controversial *Ninety-Five Theses* actually fit quite well within the guideposts of Catholic orthodoxy, which leads Hahn and Wiker to assert that, "if Martin Luther's criticisms of the Church had remained as they appeared in his ninety-five theses . . . there would likely have been no Protestant Reformation (or at least not one associated with Luther)."[28] The complicating economic and political factor was that monies for indulgences bled out of German regions and flowed to the papacy. Thus, Luther's challenges to reform on that matter of indulgences fit conveniently into German national aspirations and with anger against Rome that had been fomenting for quite some time.

Luther's turn to Scripture as sole authority (the Protestant principle of *sola Scriptura*) made earnest the search for a method to replace Catholic tradition.[29] Luther turned to the state, much like Wycliffe before him, to control the public secular realm.[30] But it was with Luther's understanding of the "priesthood of all believers" and grounding in no authority aside from Scripture, that Luther could inspire a peasant revolt.[31] *Sola fide* (justification by faith alone) became Luther's hermeneutical key for unlocking Scripture's meaning, and thus his idea of "promise" replaced the traditional role of typology.[32] Upset with justifications of papal authority from spiritual exegesis, Luther severed Scripture's intimate bond with the liturgy, and erected sharp dichotomies between the "letter" and the "spirit," the "law" and the "gospel," and, importantly, the "Old" and "New" Testaments.[33]

---

25. See, e.g., Oberman, *Dawn of the Reformation*; Oberman, *Masters of the Reformation*; and Oberman, *Harvest of Medieval Theology*.

26. Hahn and Wiker, *Politicizing the Bible*, 154–57.

27. Ibid., 154–219.

28. Ibid., 158. On this, see also Moorman, *Indulgences*.

29. Hahn and Wiker, *Politicizing the Bible*, 161–62.

30. Ibid., 168.

31. Ibid., 169.

32. Ibid., 172–83.

33. Ibid., 174–77.

Luther also developed a notion that would evolve over time within later biblical criticism, namely the idea of a "canon within the canon." He explicitly exalted the Gospel of John, St. Paul's epistles (particularly Romans, Galatians, and Ephesians), and First Peter, above all other portions of Scripture.[34] After the Reformation, later within the history of modern historical biblical criticism, exegetes would move from Luther's sifting through the canon to distinguish authentic books from less authentic (or even inauthentic) books, to sifting through individual biblical books themselves, for the authentic "kernels." However, Hahn and Wiker conclude that, "Despite Luther's intentions, playing the authority of the princes against the papacy meant inadvertently giving the authority over interpretation to the secular powers" and this removed biblical interpretation from the common man.[35] Luther's trajectory was to create an exegetical elite to define interpretation authoritatively.

King Henry VIII

Continuing within the context of the sixteenth century, we turn from Luther to King Henry VIII and the English Reformation.[36] King Henry VIII's reforming policy built upon all the influential figures who we have discussed above. This background helps lay bare the English Reformation's intellectual roots and show the ways in which this prepared the seedbed for what would germinate in historical criticism. It is often forgotten that historical criticism was born in the world of English Deism prior to entering the German academy in the eighteenth and nineteenth centuries. From the English Reformation emerged Deist biblical criticism that would later transplant itself in the academic culture of Germany in the Enlightenment and nineteenth century.

Henry VIII's "Great Matter"—that of his desire to marry Anne Boleyn—unleashed a torrent of exegesis, both in England and on the continent, over what course Henry could and should take.[37] Ultimately Henry did marry Anne and the English state annulled Henry's marriage to Catherine.[38] Hahn and Wiker point out the dramatic shift that took place with this action: "the state (rather than papal) annulment of Henry's

34. Ibid., 197–201.
35. Ibid., 217.
36. Ibid., 221–55.
37. Ibid., 231–36.
38. Ibid., 235–36.

marriage marks the turning point at which the Church *in* England be-comes the Church *of* England."[39] The evidence indicates that both Machia-velli and Marsilius exerted a strong influence on Henry's Reformation.[40] Some of the Henrician reform policies' apologists utilized Machiavelli's and Marsilius's works. Moreover, the Marsilian program of subordinating the church to the state found complete expression in Henry's state church.

René Descartes

The intellectual revolution begun in the late medieval period and carried through the sixteenth century, continued into the seventeenth century. One of the most important figures in this context, but almost completely neglected within the history of biblical scholarship, is René Descartes (1596 to 1650).[41] Descartes played an important role in effecting a great cosmological shift, wherein nature became mathematized, and geometry emerged as the primary form of rationality. Descartes laid the Bible aside in his philosophical program. This set the stage for a secular cosmos de-void of God and the supernatural, and thus the ground was prepared for a fully secular biblical hermeneutic. Descartes is a key figure in the new "focus on method" that will produce a "'mania' for *method*."[42] The upshot is that, "the new, secular political focus set forth by Marsilius and Machia-velli in the fourteenth and sixteenth centuries would finally have received a cosmological foundation in the seventeenth century . . . their politicizing of Scripture could now receive support from a new science of nature."[43]

The so-called "wars of religion" of the sixteenth and seventeenth centuries are an important context for Descartes's method, as evidenced in *Discourse on Method*.[44] The examination of Descartes's method reveals how it shaped modernity: "the *mathematization*, the *mechanization*, and the *mastery* of nature."[45] Hahn and Wiker observe, "the habitual posture of doubt ingrained by following Descartes's method will become the unques-tioned beginning point of many of the most prominent scriptural scholars

39. Ibid., 236.
40. Ibid., 236–45 and 251–55.
41. Ibid., 257–84.
42. Ibid., 258.
43. Ibid.
44. Ibid., 263–80.
45. Ibid., 267.

toward the biblical texts."[46] Rather than the text having authority, it is the method that is authoritative, judging revelation and re-constructing the text on the basis of methodological conclusions.[47]

Thomas Hobbes

Thomas Hobbes (1588 to 1679) has become increasingly recognized as an important figure within the history of biblical scholarship.[48] In many ways, Hobbes represents a synthesis of what came before: his secularized exegesis makes sense for an atomist-mechanist worldview and depends upon his influence from Descartes and Machiavelli, while his exegesis supports the kind of state Henry VIII created. Like Descartes, the context for Hobbes was one of strife, both that of the bloody Thirty Years's War and also the English Civil Wars, and thus his ostensible goal was also terrestrial peace.[49] The one area scholars by and large have neglected, with a few exceptions, is Hobbes's Epicurean background.[50]

Like Machiavelli, Hobbes understood the necessity of religion in order to maintain political power, and hence he did not eliminate religion, but rather only the fear of consequences beyond physical life and death (such fear in which religion is rooted for Hobbes). For Hobbes the state sovereign must have full control over religion within the realm; belief in life after death would undermine this.[51] In the second half of *Leviathan* is Hobbes's exegetical project wherein he interprets the Bible to support his politics and philosophy, placing all temporal and spiritual power— including exegetical authority—in the hands of the civil sovereign, and declawing the church of any real authority apart from the state.[52] Hahn and Wiker convincingly identify Hobbes's " inversion of typology": "The flow of typology, properly understood, is *forward* in the Divine economy,

---

46. Ibid., 275.

47. Ibid., 279–84.

48. See, e.g., Morrow, *Three Skeptics and the Bible*, 85–103, where I devoted an entire chapter to Hobbes. For what follows, see especially Hahn and Wiker, *Politicizing the Bible*, 258–338.

49. Hahn and Wiker, *Politicizing the Bible*, 285–86, 292, and 300.

50. Exceptions include ibid., 296–99; Springborg, "Hobbes and Epicurean Religion," 161–214; and Pacchi, "Hobbes e l'epicureismo," 54–71. An important work on the influence of Epicureanism is Wiker, *Moral Darwinism*.

51. Morrow, *Three Skeptics and the Bible*, 101–3; and Hahn and Wiker, *Politicizing the Bible*, 306–9.

52. Hahn and Wiker, *Politicizing the Bible*, 315–17 and 319–22.

toward the culmination in Christ. . . . Hobbes's typology inverted the order, flowing not toward culmination and spiritual transformation, but backward, toward the reduction to some earthly, original meaning."[53]

Baruch Spinoza

As with Hobbes, the role of Baruch Spinoza (1632 to 1677) in helping to forge modern biblical criticism is likewise better acknowledged than it previously had been.[54] In fact, Spinoza played a central role in laying out a precise historical and philological biblical method, and we will discuss Spinoza's work in more detail in the next chapter. Spinoza tried to construct a scientific biblical exegesis which, like Hobbes's hermeneutic, and like Descartes's philosophy, was an attempt to bring peace to Europe torn asunder by violence they all identified as fundamentally religious in motivation.

Spinoza's excommunication from the Dutch Sephardic Jewish community in Amsterdam remains one of the most famous and yet elusive aspects of his life. Despite his notoriety, the specific reason for his excommunication remains uncertain. Hahn and Wiker simply state that Spinoza had doubts about Judaism and "embraced the radical philosophy that would lead to his expulsion from the synagogue even while his father was still alive, but out of deference to him, kept it to himself."[55] This is not patently clear by the evidence, although it is certainly possible and is perhaps the majority view among Spinoza scholars. The important work of Odette Vlessing, however, has made a very strong case that Spinoza's excommunication could be explained quite apart from philosophical or theological positions.[56] Regardless of the specific details, it is clear that Spinoza eventually moved into such a skeptical position, and that his work belongs to a much broader intellectual current, inspired in part by Cartesian philosophy, within the Dutch republic. Although Spinoza certainly applies his own radicalized brand of Cartesian skepticism to Scripture, the primary corrosive acid Spinoza employs, in sharp contrast to his Cartesian

---

53. Ibid., 334.

54. See, e.g., Morrow, *Three Skeptics and the Bible*, 104–38; and Hahn and Wiker, *Politicizing the Bible*, 339–93.

55. Hahn and Wiker, *Politicizing the Bible*, 342.

56. E.g., Vlessing, "Excommunication of Baruch Spinoza," 15–47; and Vlessing, "Jewish Community in Transition," 195–211. This is also the position of Travis Frampton (who follows Vlessing) in his *Spinoza and the Rise of Historical Criticism*.

friend Lodewijk Meyer, is history. For this, Spinoza is more directly in-debted to Francis Bacon than to Descartes.[57]

Spinoza's *Ethics* is a crucial hermeneutical key for correctly reading Spinoza. Once it becomes clear, as in *Ethics*, that God *is* nature, then it becomes clear that miracles are impossible.[58] The scientific exegete hence must find an alternative explanation for the common occurrences of mir-acles in Scripture.[59] Ironically, this is precisely what Machiavelli did before Spinoza, which should come as no surprise since, as Graham Hammill notes, Spinoza was "one of Machiavelli's most perceptive readers."[60]

Richard Simon

Another important figure, to whom we will return in chapter 3 of this book, is Richard Simon (1638 to 1712).[61] Simon hoped to defend Catholic tradition and at the same time demolish the Protestant assumption of *sola Scriptura*.[62] In order to do so, however, Simon took Spinoza's arguments even further, multiplying problems with the biblical text, as we shall show more thoroughly in chapter 3.[63] Simon's approach of accepting and cel-ebrating surface incongruities in the Bible rather than trying to explain seeming imperfections as containing hidden perfections was quite novel within the Catholic tradition at that point in time. For Simon, apparent mistakes in the text indicated the absolute need for *traditio*.[64] And yet Si-mon's use of tradition appeared arbitrary.[65]

---

57. Bacon is important for understanding Spinoza. Unfortunately, there is very little treatment in the scholarly literature of Bacon's role in Spinoza's method, despite the fact that Spinoza read Bacon, and included in his method a historical method that clearly attempted (even to the point of linguistic parallels to Bacon's work) to bring Bacon's history of nature to bear on a history of Scripture. Much more scholarship needs to be devoted to this neglected influence. For the role of Bacon on Spinoza, see, e.g., Preus, *Spinoza and the Irrelevance of Biblical Authority*, 7n19, 24n73, 26n80, 38, 158n9, 159, 159n12, 161–68, 163nn20–21, 181, and 195; Gabbey, "Spinoza's Natural Science," 170–72; and Zac, *Spinoza et l'interprétation*, 29–37.

58. Hahn and Wiker, *Politicizing the Bible*, 364–65.

59. Ibid., 365.

60. Hammill, *Mosaic Constitution*, 22.

61. Hahn and Wiker, *Politicizing the Bible*, 395–423.

62. Ibid., 396–400.

63. Ibid., 396–400 and 404–23.

64. Ibid., 398.

65. Ibid., 399, 405, 410–12, 416–18, and 422.

Simon's reception ensured that his work and that the method of Spinoza would survive into the eighteenth century and beyond.[66] Simon's work was received warmly in England by John Locke (1632 to 1704) and some of the Deists, and his work was likewise read and became influential in Germany, among Gottfried Wilhelm Leibniz (1646 to 1716), Johann David Michaelis (1717 to 1791)—whom we will discuss more thoroughly in chapter 4 of this present volume—and Johann Salomo Semler (1725 to 1791), among others. An examination of Simon's *Histoire critique du Vieux Testament*[67] and of his *Histoire critique du text du Nouveau Testament*[68] highlights that, "Simon shifted the focus of biblical studies from the substance of the text to the history of the text."[69] Simon also posited "a layered editorial history" for Scripture.[70] Thus emerges one necessity of a skilled scholarly exegete in order to make sense of the tattered threads of Scripture.[71]

John Locke

As mentioned above, Simon's work was received by and influenced Locke, who in turn became an important yet neglected figure within the history of modern biblical criticism.[72] The English Civil Wars form the important context for Locke's work. Locke was about ten years old when this First Civil War erupted, and his family was on the side represented by Parliament, which was basically "the new propertied class."[73] The Second Civil War found Locke at Westminster School, age fifteen.[74] Locke was studying at Oxford during the tumultuous transition from the Third Civil War and the chaos which ensued to Oliver Cromwell's military rule.[75]

This context of violent strife and the "nearly anarchic radicalism" that was rampant throughout England profoundly shaped Locke, who

66. Ibid., 400–4.
67. See ibid., 404–12.
68. See ibid., 412–22.
69. Ibid., 404.
70. Ibid., 405–6.
71. Ibid., 413.
72. Ibid., 425–86.
73. Ibid., 426–27.
74. Ibid., 427–28.
75. Ibid., 428.

proved himself "deeply influenced" by Hobbes's *Leviathan*.[76] Locke's political machinations forced him into exile as he was trailed by royal spies on the continent.[77] As a Whig, Locke was constantly involved in political plots and intrigue, including a plan for violent rebellion. Locke may have been personally involved in the Rye House Plot, a plan to kidnap and then murder King Charles II (whom Locke earlier supported) and the king's brother.[78]

In self-imposed exile Locke remained in the Dutch Republic, where he was exposed to radical intellectual traditions, including Jean Le Clerc (1657 to 1736), the critic of Richard Simon, who would become a good friend of Locke's.[79] Like Spinoza, a core morality, which has been obscured by so much attention to doctrine, became Scripture's central message for Locke.[80] For Locke, "Rather than Scripture taking believers into the heart of profound mystery, where the actual *events* of sacred history reveal, as types, eternal and supernatural truths, the Bible became a kind of morality manual that, at its best, illustrated merely rational moral truths."[81] Locke's vision of toleration required a secular governing authority and the complete privatization of religion.[82]

Locke's *An Essay Concerning Human Understanding* holds an important place within his overall epistemology and fits within Locke's overarching political plan.[83] Locke is privatizing faith, while uniting Cartesian rationalism with the empiricism of science. In the *Essay Concerning Human Understanding*, Locke seeks to limit reason's abilities, and then expand the power and capability of this new anemic reason. For Locke reason has to do with "*our* clear and distinct ideas," and thus it is capable of judging revelation. If something cannot be clearly "sensed," if it "is beyond sense," then it is nothing but utter "nonsense."[84] We can see how with Locke, "The principle of *sola scriptura* was therefore transformed into the principle *sola ratio*."[85]

---

76. Ibid., 426–33.
77. Ibid., 440–41.
78. Ibid.
79. Ibid., 441–44, 454, and 476–77.
80. Ibid., 446.
81. Ibid., 447.
82. Ibid., 448.
83. Ibid., 450.
84. Ibid., 451.
85. Ibid., 452.

Locke's scriptural work was intended to minimize faith commitments to the barest minimum possible in order to further his political goals. Indeed, his *The Reasonableness of Christianity* basically boils down to an apologetic for the notion that the only really important thing for which Scripture demands the adherence of faith is that Jesus was in fact the Messiah.[86] With such a doctrinal reduction, there would no longer be any reason for violent religious controversies. The important thing for Locke was "civic morality."[87] Hahn and Wiker sum up Locke's entire interpretive goal: "Jesus was reduced to being the Messiah so He could be a lawmaker–king, a miracle worker who confirmed the authority of morality for those incapable of philosophical demonstration . . . his [Locke] main interest seems to be the utility of the Bible for keeping political order."[88]

John Toland

So many of the skeptical conclusions of late eighteenth and nineteenth century historical critics were already firmly in place in the seventeenth century in the work of John Toland (1670 to 1722), who relied upon works of many of the figures we covered above.[89] In his 1704 *Letters to Serena*, Toland establishes a "method of equivocation" in his notion of "two doctrines," the idea that the enlightened philosopher must hide some things from the more ignorant masses. Toland continued his "method of equivocation" in his 1720 *Pantheisticon* which attempted to explain Toland's pantheism. In it he clearly called for the enlightened philosopher to separate from the masses.[90] Such an enlightened philosopher could "talk" with the people in the crowds, but must only "think" with other enlightened philosophers.[91]

Like Spinoza and Machiavelli before him, Toland put forward natural explanations to eliminate any apparent miracle in Scripture. Any explanation would do so long as it was natural and not mysterious or supernatural.[92] For Toland, reason alone was sufficient to understand Scripture, which must be studied as any other book. Moreover, since there was

86. Ibid., 468.
87. Ibid., 471.
88. Ibid., 472.
89. Ibid., 487–541.
90. Ibid., 489.
91. Ibid., 490.
92. Ibid., 526.

no supernatural, no miracles, nothing mysterious, there was no need for priesthood nor priestly mediation. His assumptions here would govern the rest of modern historical criticism, with its transformation of the Bible into a book like any other, its refusal to allow for the supernatural and instead seeking out a natural, any natural, explanation in its place, and its view of priesthood as a devolution or corruption of what came before.[93] Toland, as with later historical critical exegetes, would "reformulate history in terms of degeneration from rational religion to priestly superstition."[94] Hahn and Wiker demonstrate how Toland was "part of a larger, radical international intellectual movement that had rejected Christianity."[95]

The historical-critical method continued to develop in the eighteenth and nineteenth centuries grounded on the foundations I described above. More work needs to be done showing the ways in which the history discussed in this chapter plays out in the later centuries, with the names more often associated with historical biblical criticism: Gotthold Ephraim Lessing (1729 to 1781), Hermann Samuel Reimarus (1694 to 1768), David Friedrich Strauss (1808 to 1874), Johann Salomo Semler (1725 to 1791), Johann Jakob Griesbach (1745 to 1812), Johann Gottfried Eichhorn (1752 to 1827), Wilhelm Martin Leberecht de Wette (1780 to 1849), Heinrich Julius Holtzmann (1832 to 1910), and Julius Wellhausen (1844 to 1918).[96] Surveying this history, however, I arrive at the same conclusion as Hahn and Wiker, namely that "the radical conclusions of the historical-critical method were built into the method itself."[97]

In the next chapter, I will look more carefully at the work of Spinoza, situating his exegesis in its historical and political context. In my prior work, *Three Skeptics and the Bible*, I devoted a chapter to Spinoza, focusing on his social and historical context, and discussing the outline of his programmatic method for biblical scholarship.[98] In the next chapter, chapter 2, I look more specifically at his exegesis. The example I use is Spinoza's interpretations of the Psalms in his *Tractatus theologico-politicus*. This shows how his exegesis functioned within his overarching politics.

93. Ibid., 532–33.
94. Ibid., 533.
95. Ibid., 505.
96. Scott Hahn and I are currently at work on just such a volume.
97. Hahn and Wiker, *Politicizing the Bible*, 487.
98. See Morrow, *Three Skeptics and the Bible*, 104–38.

2

THE PSALTER AND SEVENTEENTH CENTURY POLITICS

Spinoza's *Theological-Political Treatise*

As WE SAW IN the last chapter, Baruch Spinoza (1632 to 1677) stands in an important place within the history of modern biblical criticism.[1] In this chapter, I take a look at a specific instance of his exegesis, namely his use of Psalms, in his controversial 1670 work *Tractatus theologico-politicus*. Spinoza's *Tractatus theologico-politicus* is primarily known as a work of political philosophy, and yet much of Spinoza's text addresses matters of biblical exegesis. In fact, his entire seventh chapter is devoted to laying out a method for how to interpret the Bible scientifically.[2]

In this chapter I examine Spinoza's use of the Book of Psalms throughout his *Tractatus theologico-politicus*, showing how the specific psalms he selects function within his apologetic framework in defense of his political philosophy. In some instances, the psalms serve to naturalize what Jews and Christians traditionally considered the supernatural. In other places, Spinoza uses the psalms to support one or more aspects of Spinoza's concept of God in the *Tractatus theologico-politicus*.[3] Particularly

1. See Morrow, *Three Skeptics and the Bible*, 104–38.

2. Unless otherwise mentioned, all citations to Spinoza's *Tractatus theologico-politicus* will be taken from (Spinoza, *Theological–Political Treatise*). Anytime, however, that the Latin text is being consulted, those citations and quotation will be coming from the most recent critical edition (Spinoza, *Tractatus theologico–politicus*).

3. This is as distinct from the way in which Spinoza describes God in his *Ethica*.

illuminating is Spinoza's use of Psalm 40 in the *Tractatus theologico–politi-cus's* fifth chapter, which pertains to the role religious ceremonies play in the Bible. Spinoza redeploys Psalm 40 in order to deemphasize the impor-tance of external ritual. In doing this, Spinoza resembles certain strains of Protestant exegesis from the previous hundred years or more, and the traditions of interpretation they bequeathed. As we shall see, this use of Psalm 40 serves an important function within Spinoza's overall political philosophy, wherein he asserts the authority of the state on all matters pertaining to the public realm, including religious ceremonies and rituals. Although Spinoza cites portions of the Pentateuch more frequently than the Psalms, out of the 74 different sources Spinoza explicitly cites through-out his *Tractatus theologico–politicus* (see Tables 1–14),[4] only six are cited more frequently than the Psalms, making the Psalms one of the most im-portant sources upon which Spinoza relies, and the most important from among the wisdom literature of the Old Testament (see Tables 1–6).[5]

The Historical Context for Spinoza's Use of Psalms

As we saw in the first chapter, Spinoza stands in a pivotal place within the history of the march toward modern biblical criticism—the sort of biblical criticism that would come to full flower in the German universities of the later eighteenth and nineteenth centuries.[6] This progressive development of modern biblical criticism, extending back into the medieval period, participated in and was affected by the major cultural currents and shifts

---

Spinoza began his *Ethica* prior to writing *Tractatus theologico-politicus*, but interrupted his work in order to publish the latter. After publishing *Tractatus theologico-politicus*, Spinoza completed his *Ethica*, but without publishing it. Although Spinoza's discus-sions of God in *Tractatus theologico-politicus* are easier to square with more traditional Jewish and Christian conceptions, his descriptions of God in *Ethica*, wherein God is collapsed into nature, are not.

4. Throughout this chapter reference will be made to sixteen tables which appear at the end of this chapter.

5. Spinoza makes an explicit reference to Baruch, which seems to be a reference to the Book of Baruch, but it is possible he is simply referencing Baruch as Jeremiah's scribe and not to the actual text of Baruch, in which case, Spinoza only cites from seventy-three different sources. With the exception of the Bible, whose authorship is highly contested, I am using sources to refer to authors. Thus in some cases, he is rely-ing upon multiple works by the same author. With regard to biblical books, I count each book as a different source.

6. Morrow, *Three Skeptics and the Bible*, 10–53; and Goshen-Gottstein, "Textual Criticism," 376.

taking place historically throughout Europe.[7] Medieval debates about the relationship between throne and altar, which resulted in many conflicts, were aided by the court exegesis performed by Marsilius of Padua and William of Ockham, whose exegesis was motivated and shaped by the very debates their work served.[8] The Renaissance and Humanist emphasis *ad fontes*, which we find in Machiavelli as well as Erasmus, emphasized the honing of philological and textual skills to the finest point possible.[9] The Protestant Reformation's singular emphasis on the text of Scripture, particularly in contrast to the authority of popes and councils, combined these prior trends of philological and textual focus, taking them in a direction that was greatly influenced by the politics of its time.[10]

The work of Martin Luther in particular coincided with German princes's desires for autonomy from the Papal States.[11] This wish for political autonomy was not a unique German desire, but was widespread throughout Europe in regions that remained Catholic after the Reformation, as well as in regions where the Protestant Reformation was successful. Indeed, every region that remained Catholic after the Reformation had already managed to secure concordat agreements with the pope, prior to the Reformation. These agreements limited papal authority within their realms, especially by the state appointment of bishops and the curbing of monies that bled out of their realms to the Papal States. In contrast, the Protestant Reformation only succeeded in regions that failed to secure such concordats in advance. Thus, the practicalities of both the enduring presence of Catholicism in places like France, as well as the success of Protestantism in places like the Germanic regions, functioned as ideological justifications for increasing state sovereignty and as means of limiting the pope's reach within their realms.[12] R. W. Scribner and C. Scott Dixon's

---

7. Morrow, chapter 1 in this present volume; Morrow, "Averroism, Nominalism, and Mechanization," 1293–1340; and Hahn and Wiker, *Politicizing the Bible.*

8. Hahn and Wiker, *Politicizing the Bible*, 17–59; and Minnis, "Material Swords," 292–308. On the complexity of the social order in the medieval period, see Jones, *Before Church and State.*

9. Legaspi, *Death of Scripture*, 10–22; Kugel, "Bible in the University," 143–65; Goshen–Gottstein, "Foundations of Biblical Philology," 77–94; and Goshen–Gottstein, "Christianity," 69–88.

10. Hahn and Wiker, *Politicizing the Bible*, 147–219; and Frampton, *Spinoza and the Rise of Historical Criticism*, 23–42.

11. Hahn and Wiker, *Politicizing the Bible*, 154–57 and 159–68.

12. Cavanaugh, *Myth of Religious Violence*, 166–67; Cavanaugh, "Fire Strong Enough," 400–401; and Skinner, *Foundations of Modern Political Thought 2*, 59–60.

comments on the Reformation's immediate aftermath are illuminating here:

> After a brief period of mass enthusiasm, . . . [support for the Reformation] retreated to being a minority phenomenon. At a crude estimate, during the first generation of the Reformation, up to mid-century, and perhaps even during the second, probably no more than 10 percent of the German population ever showed an active and lasting enthusiasm for reformed ideas. Where massive numbers were "won" after 1526, to what became the new church, it occurred involuntarily, through a prince deciding that his territory should adopt the new faith. When we speak of the extensive hold "Protestantism" had on Germany by the second half of the sixteenth century . . . this was because there were large numbers of "involuntary Protestants" created by the princes' confessional choices.[13]

Spinoza stands firmly within this stream. Although he comes from a Sephardic Jewish background, his tendencies are more toward a Protestant-informed exegesis than a traditional Jewish one. Such tendencies were more a matter of circumstance and situation than enthusiasm. Spinoza's exegetical work and methodological program in his *Tractatus theologico-politicus* is also pivotal in taking this exegesis further, secularizing it in Spinoza's ostensible intent to create a scientific biblical exegesis patterned on the then emerging natural sciences.[14] Spinoza's political concern to avoid Church-court politics, however, were at the forefront of his mind, and were explicit in his work, as he made clear when he wrote in the preface of his *Tractatus theologico-politicus*:

> As I reflected on all this . . . that doctrinal conflicts are fought out in Church and Court with intense passion and generate the most bitter antipathies and struggles, which quickly bring men to sedition, as well as a whole host of other things that it would take too long to explain here—I resolved in all seriousness to make a fresh examination of Scripture with a free and

13. Scribner and Dixon, *German Reformation*, 34. Compare this with the history of the Reformation in Duffy, *Voices of Morebath*; and Duffy, *Stripping of the Altars*.

14. Morrow, *Three Skeptics and the Bible*, 104–38. Thus his important, but often unrecognized, use of Francis Bacon's method (Manrique Charry, "La herencia de Bacon," 121–30; Morrow, *Three Skeptics and the Bible*, 118–19; Preus, *Spinoza and the Irrelevance of Biblical Authority*, 38, 161–68, 181, and 195; and Zac, *Spinoza et l'interprétation*, 29–32).

unprejudiced mind . . . . With this proviso in mind, I devised a
method for interpreting the sacred volumes.[15]

We should bear in mind that by this point, Spinoza had been kicked
out of the Sephardic Jewish community of Amsterdam, for reasons not en-
tirely known.[16] He befriended a number of intellectuals who remained on
the margins of the reigning Calvinist orthodoxy within the Dutch Republic, and often quite outside the bounds of that orthodoxy.[17] His *Tractatus
theologico-politicus* was an attempt to eviscerate the traditional authority
of religious traditions, and then repackage those traditions so that on all
external matters they would be seen as subservient to the state—and all of
this on the basis of the Scriptural texts held so dearly by Jewish and Christian traditions. Spinoza's historical exegesis was an ostensible attempt to
level the playing field, as it were, giving everyone equal access to the Bible's
meaning. In reality, it privileged the emerging secular states, and the future secular exegetical specialists envisioned by such a method, over and
against any and every religious tradition unwilling to secularize.[18] This
was by design.

Spinoza's Use of Psalms in His
Tractatus Theologico-Politicus

In examining Spinoza's use of Psalms, I follow the order in which he brings
them up in his book. His exegetical approach to Psalms in general, within

---

15. Spinoza, *Theological–Political Treatise*, 8–9.

16. Kaplan, "Social Functions," 111–55; Popkin, *Spinoza*, 27–38; and Vlessing, "Excommunication of Baruch Spinoza," 15–47. One of the possible reasons for his excommunication that is too little considered, despite the impressive archival evidence that
lends it credence, pertains to the combination of Spinoza's defaming his father who had
been a prominent member of the synagogue community, blaming his late father for
the financial debt Spinoza owed, and then Spinoza's securing a legal gentile guardian
from the secular Amsterdam authorities, thereby bypassing the Jewish authorities who
would normally deal with the financial situation. Spinoza's act cancelled his debt and
would have been seen as a major public embarrassment to the Sephardic Jewish community of Amsterdam at that time. See Morrow, *Three Skeptics and the Bible*, 104–38;
Frampton, *Spinoza and the Rise of Historical Criticism*, 141–47 and 153; Vlessing, "Excommunication of Baruch Spinoza," 15–47; Vlessing, "Jewish Community," 195–211;
Vlessing, "New Light," 43–75; and Kaplan, "Social Functions," 111–55.

17. Popkin, "Some New Light," 171–88; Popkin, "Spinoza and Samuel Fisher,"
219–36; Popkin, "Spinoza's Relations," 14–28; and Popkin, "Spinoza, the Quakers and
the Millenarians," 113–33.

18. Levenson, *Hebrew Bible*, 117–25.

his *Tractatus theologico-politicus*, is not systematic in approach, but rather Spinoza uses and interprets the Psalms in passing, in order to bolster his arguments. Although Spinoza's citations of the Psalms only account for 3 percent of his total overall citations, and 4 percent of his citations from the Old Testament, the Psalms (along with 1 Samuel) remain the seventh most frequently cited source out of seventy-four sources (see Tables 1–14), and the sixth most frequently cited Old Testament book (see Tables 1–6).[19] The first time Spinoza brings up Psalms explicitly is in *Tractatus theologico-politicus*'s first chapter, "On Prophecy." He cites Psalm 135 as evidence that the Hebrew word *ruach*, often translated as "spirit," can be used to mean a variety of natural phenomena, in this case "breath." Spinoza writes, "The word *ruagh* in its literal sense means 'wind' . . . but it is very often used to refer to many other things, all of them, however, derived from 'wind'. It is used: (1) to signify 'breath', as in Psalm 135.17, 'also there is no spirit in their mouth.'"[20] Although it is obviously the case that *ruach* can mean "wind" or "breath," Spinoza only includes natural meanings in his discussion here.[21]

This proves significant, because Spinoza offers a very thorough and erudite discussion of "spirit" using both Hebrew *ruach* and its Latin equivalent *spiritus* in ways that are vastly different from how they have been traditionally interpreted and translated.[22] Spinoza isolates seven major

19. If we include Spinoza's citations of sources in his later marginal annotations that were intended to be incorporated into later editions of the *Tractatus theologico-politicus*, the citations of Psalms remains 3 percent of the overall citations, and 4 percent of the Old Testament citations (see Tables 1–14). The only difference is that 1 Samuel displaces Psalms as the seventh most cited source and sixth from the Old Testament. Whereas in the actual text of Spinoza's *Tractatus theologico-politicus* both 1 Samuel and the Psalms are cited twenty-five times, Spinoza did not add any citations from the Psalms in his marginal annotations, but he did add a further two citations from 1 Samuel (see Tables 1–6).

20. Spinoza, *Theological-Political Treatise*, 20. In Latin, *Spiritus* can likewise be "spirit" or "breath."

21. The possible exception here is when he includes the notion of "soul." Whether or not this is natural or supernatural depends on whether one views the soul as a natural or supernatural entity. See the important study on Spinoza's philological analysis of *ruach* in his *Tractatus theologico-politicus* as a challenge to Maimonides' hermeneutic in his *Guide to the Perplexed* (Diamond, "Maimonides, Spinoza, and Buber," 320–43, esp. 328–36). Shortly after this discussion, Spinoza alludes to a passage in Psalms (presumably Psalm 80:10) which references the "cedars of God" (21). The context here is explaining "cedars of God," apparently God's possessions, as, in this case referring rather to their "extraordinary height" (21).

22. See Tables 15–16 for Spinoza's use of "spirit" in his *Tractatus theologico-politicus*. One of the most important examinations of Spinoza's linguistic discussion of "spirit" to

categories for how "spirit" should be understood in the Bible: "breath"; "life"; "courage"/"strength"; "ability"; "mind"; "soul"; "quarters of the world."[23] As can be seen from Table 16, Spinoza will define "spirit" in more than thirty different ways, all of which fall into one or more of the above seven categories. Most often, Spinoza understands "spirit" as having to do with the "mind" (see Table 16). Spinoza employs the word "spirit," referring either to God or to his linguistic discussion about "spirit" in order to understand the idea of "spirit of God," 148 times in his *Tractatus theologico-politicus* (see Table 15). He only explicitly defines the word sixty-three of those times, 42.5 percent of the times that he uses the phrase (see Tables 15–16).[24] In some cases, Spinoza writes, "'spirit of God' and 'spirit of Jehovah', signify nothing more . . . than an extremely violent, very dry and fatal wind."[25]

Proceeding further in chapter 1, Spinoza comes to Psalm 51 wherein he marshals this famous penitential psalm to support his interpretation that the *ruach* of God can be understood, in passages, to refer to "the

---

date is Diamond, "Maimonides, Spinoza, and Buber," 328–36. Not all of Spinoza's new uses of "spirit" are completely unique to his work, since Hobbes already engaged in a similar comparison in his *Leviathan* with which Spinoza was likely familiar. But, unlike Hobbes, who did not know Hebrew, Spinoza was able to place these new uses of "spirit" on more solid philological ground. For a brief look at Hobbes's interpretation of "spirit" in the Bible see Morrow, *Three Skeptics and the Bible*, 100–101. On Spinoza's knowledge of Hobbes see Parkin, "Reception of Hobbes's *Leviathan*," 450–51; Malcolm, *Aspects of Hobbes*, 390–92; Pacchi, "*Leviathan* and Spinoza's *Tractatus*," 577; Osier, "L'herméneutique de Hobbes," 319–47; Schumann, "Methodenfragen bei Spinoza," 47–86; and Sacksteder, "How Much of Hobbes," 25–39.

23. Spinoza, *Theological–Political Treatise*, 20–26.

24. As can be seen from Table 15, part of the reason for this is that 25.6 percent (thirty-eight times) of his use of "spirit" is simply Spinoza's use of *ruach* in Hebrew font as part of a quotation from the Old Testament. A further 24.3 percent (thirty-six times) of his use of "spirit" represents Spinoza's use of the Latin *spiritus* as a translation of these Old Testament quotations. In another 10.1 percent (fifteen times) of the cases, Spinoza is providing a Hebrew phrase (not tied explicitly to a specific verse from the Old Testament) in Hebrew font. In yet another 10.1 percent (fifteen times) of these instances, Spinoza is providing a Latin translation of these Hebrew phrases. Finally, in 3 percent (five times) of his uses of "spirit" Spinoza is merely transliterating the Hebrew word, which he just printed in Hebrew font, into Latin letters. Adding up the percentages here yields more than 100 percent, the reason being that in some of the instances cited above in this footnote Spinoza does actually explain what he means by "spirit." The point is that many of these examples do not require explanation, e.g., when Spinoza lists the word "spirit" in Hebrew font, and then transliterates it, or when he quotes from a biblical passage in Hebrew, and then translates it into Latin. In many of these instances, he is using the term "spirit" but simply transliterating or translating a passage or phrase for an audience that might not be literate in Hebrew.

25. Spinoza, *Theological-Political Treatise*, 22.

human mind itself."[26] He observes: "So also Psalm 51.12–13, 'create in me a clean heart, O God, and renew in me a proper' (or, modest) 'spirit' (i.e., desire)."[27] Rather than "spirit," however, Spinoza sees *ruach* as referencing the human mind.

Spinoza then underscores what he detects to be anthropomorphisms in Scripture regarding depictions of God. He explains, "Now, since Scripture, deferring to the limitations of the common people, is accustomed to depict God like a man, and to ascribe to God a mind and a heart and the passions of the heart, as well as body and breath, 'the spirit of God' is often used in the Bible for mind, i.e., heart, passion, force and the breath of the mouth of God."[28] Thus, Ps 143:10 refers to the mind of God, and Ps 33:6 "improperly" attributes breath of God.[29] Writing further, and quoting (but not naming) Ps 33:6, Spinoza claims, "the Psalmist, speaking poetically, even says, 'by the command of God the heavens were made, and all their host by the spirit' or breath 'of his mouth' (i.e. by his decree, as if it were expressed as a breath)."[30] Spinoza likewise interprets God's spirit in Ps 139:7 as figurative.[31] Neither human beings, nor God, it seems have a supernaturally understood "spirit," according to Spinoza.

This naturalization of spirit is crucial for Spinoza's broader Machiavellian project of unmasking the assumed hidden political agenda of religions and of hypocritical religious leaders. As we read regarding Machiavelli in one recent work:

> The gap between the appearance of holiness and the underlying reality of corruption in the Curia became, for Machiavelli, the paradigmatic form of princely deception. . . . Machiavelli inferred that the same gap exists in the biblical text itself. His discovery of the "key" to the underlying motives of biblical figures created a new mode of exegesis, and Machiavelli therefore

---

26. Ibid., 23.

27. Ibid. He finishes the quotation, "Do not cast me away from your sight, nor take the mind of your holiness from me," and then comments, "Because sins were believed to arise from the flesh alone, and the mind was believed to urge nothing but good, he invokes the help of God against the desires of the flesh, but for the mind which the holy God gave him, he only prays God to preserve it."

28. Ibid.

29. Ibid.

30. Ibid., 24.

31. Ibid.

can rightly be considered as one of the earliest, and certainly the most influential, sources of the hermeneutics of suspicion.[32]

From this view, much of what is merely natural in the Bible has been interpreted supernaturally as a tool of priestcraft. Such pretensions must be unmasked, and when the veil is taken away, such tyrannical religious powers will be rendered impotent and thus religious strife will end and peace will reign on the earth, or so the view goes. Replacing "spirit" with "mind" is one way of delegitimizing those authorities concerned with the supernatural spirit; without "spirit," state leaders can guide all actions toward the end of earthly peace, concerned with the human mind rather than human spirit.

In Spinoza's third chapter, "On the vocation of the Hebrews, and whether the prophetic gift was peculiar to them," Spinoza uses the Psalms to defend the notion that all people are equal under God:

> For the Psalmist says (Psalm 145.8), "God is near to all those who call upon him, to all who call upon him in truth." Likewise at 145.9, "God is kind to all men, and his mercy is to all things that he had made." At Psalm 33.15 it is plainly stated that God gave the same intellect to all men, in these words, "who forms their heart in the same manner." For the heart was believed by the Hebrews to be the seat of the soul and of the intellect, as I suppose is well enough known to everyone.[33]

As with the naturalization of spirit, this chapter naturalizes prophecy and discredits the notion of a people chosen by God. In so doing, Spinoza uses these texts to discredit religious authority which rests so much on allegedly prophetic and divinely inspired revelation given to a particular people. Here, Spinoza uses the Psalms to internationalize and universalize God's designs for humanity. He attempts to undercut Jewish claims to the unique calling of the Hebrew people in the Hebrew Bible. At the same time, this implicitly undercuts any Christian claims to unique status as new Israel.

It is in the fifth chapter, however, that we find one of the most significant tactics undertaken by Spinoza in his use of the Psalms. He entitled this fifth chapter, "On the reason why ceremonies were instituted, and on belief in the historical narratives, i.e. for what reason and for whom such belief is necessary." We get a very clear sense of Spinoza's program here by how he employs Psalm 40:

32. Hahn and Wiker, *Politicizing the Bible*, 144.
33. Spinoza, *Theological–Political Treatise*, 49.

Equally lucid is the testimony of verses 7–9 of Psalm 40, where the Psalmist says to God: "Sacrifice and offering you did not wish, you have opened your ears to me, you have not sought a holocaust and an offering for sin; I have sought to carry out your will, O God; for your law is in my entrails." Thus he applies the term "law of God" only to what is inscribed in the entrails or heart, and excludes ceremonies from it; for ceremonies are good only by convention and not by nature, and therefore are not inscribed in the heart. Other passages in Scripture testify to the same thing, but it is enough to refer to these two [the other being Isa 1].[34]

Spinoza maintains that, according to Scripture, the law of God is primarily internal, and that external ceremonies and rituals are the purview of the state. Following Isaiah 58, and using the Psalms as support, Spinoza explains further:

Thus we see that the prophet promises as the reward for liberating [the oppressed] and practicing charity, a healthy mind in a healthy body and the glory of God after death, but the reward for ceremonies is merely the security of the state, prosperity, and worldly success. In Psalms 15 and 24 no mention is made of ceremonies, but only of moral teaching, evidently because in these psalms only happiness is proposed and offered, albeit in figurative language. For it is certain that in these psalms the "mountain of God" and "God's tents" and living in them signifies happiness and peace of mind, not the mountain of Jerusalem or the tabernacle of Moses; for no one lived in these places, and they were served by men from the tribe of Levi alone.[35]

Judaism and the Church therefore may offer a "moral teaching," but their ceremonies and rituals are clearly inessential to the practice of the faith.

This use of the Psalms represents Spinoza's clearest attempt to redeploy the Psalms to privatize religion. It is part of Spinoza's rant against external ceremony. Very strong elements of this were present in certain segments of the Protestant Reformation,[36] as well as in Spinoza's contemporaries like Thomas Hobbes.[37] Spinoza radicalizes it beyond any of the Reformers, such that no external rites, ceremonies, sacraments, etc., have

34. Ibid., 69.

35. Ibid., 70–71.

36. Gregory, *Unintended Reformation*, 25–178; and Asad, *Genealogies of Religion*, 28, 39, and 58.

37. Morrow, *Three Skeptics and the Bible*, 85–103 and 139–49.

any value before God, but rather remain squarely within the purview of
the state. The state, for which God apparently has no concern, thus maintains absolute control over such external matters as religious ceremonies.

In his sixth chapter, "On miracles," he makes a passing parenthetical
reference to Psalm 73 that does not have much import, but more significantly for chapter six, and for his continued efforts throughout the *Tractatus theologico-politicus* to naturalize the supernatural, Spinoza invokes
Pss 104, 105, and 147, in order to emphasize that so called miracles are
really natural phenomena and not miraculous at all.[38] Spinoza claims that,
"when the Bible says that this or that was done by God or by the will of
God, it simply means that it was done according to the laws and order of
nature, and not, as most people think, that nature ceased to operate for a
time or that its order was briefly interrupted."[39] Thus he writes:

> In Psalm 105.24 it is stated that God turned the hearts of the
> Egyptians to hate the Israelites; this too was a natural change
> . . . . At Psalm 147.18 the natural action and heat of the wind
> by which frost and snow are melted is termed the word of God,
> and in verse 15 wind and cold are called the utterance and word
> of God. In Psalm 104.4 wind and fire are styled the envoys and
> ministers of God, and there are many other things in the Bible
> to this effect, showing very clearly that the decree of God, his
> command, his utterance, his word are nothing other than the
> very action and order of nature.[40]

In support that nature is fixed and ordered, by natural laws, Spinoza invokes Ps 148:6.[41] Thus Spinoza transfers that which was traditionally understood as the intentional work of God to the scripted work of nature.[42]

---

38. Hammill, *Mosaic Constitution*, 72–81; James, *Spinoza on Philosophy*, 139–84;
Nadler, *Book Forged in Hell*, 76–103; Rosenthal, "Miracles," 231; Garrido Zaragoza, "La
desmitificación," 3–45; and Popkin, "Hume and Spinoza," 87–89.

39. Spinoza, *Theological–Political Treatise*, 89.

40. Ibid., 89–90.

41. Ibid., 95.

42. In the tenth chapter, "Where the remaining books of the Old Testament are
examined in the same manner as the earlier ones," we find Spinoza's very brief historical
treatment of the Psalms' background. He writes, "The Psalms too were collected and
divided into five books in the period of the Second Temple. According to Philo Judaeus,
Psalm 88 was published when King Jehoiakim was still in prison in Babylon, and Psalm
89 after the same king had regained his liberty, something I do not think Philo would
have said, were it not either the received opinion of his time or had he not received it
from others worthy of credence" (ibid., 144–45).

Finally, in Spinoza's seventeenth chapter, we find a very brief reference to Ps 139:21–22, to explain why Israelites might have thought it was pious to consider others as enemies of God.[43] This chapter bears the very lengthy title: "Where it is shown that no one can transfer all things to the sovereign power, and that it is not necessary to do so; on the character of the Hebrew state in the time of Moses, and in the period after his death before the appointment of the kings; on its excellence, and on the reasons why this divine state could perish, and why it could scarcely exist without sedition." Spinoza hence indicates that the Hebrew state, despite temporary success, was destined for failure. Thus, he continues his attempt to delegitimize the notion of Israel as God's chosen people, and likewise, emphasize that the so-called Laws of God were only state laws for the particular Hebrew state while it existed.

In the end, we find that Spinoza's use of the Psalms is selective, as is his use of other portions of the Bible; he chooses those which support his political designs. In order to secure the freedom to philosophize, Spinoza has to neutralize the religious authorities that are unwilling to privatize their traditions: particularly Catholics, Calvinists, and Jews in the seventeenth century Dutch Republic. Spinoza's overall biblical exegesis in the *Tractatus theologico-politicus*, including his use of these Psalms discussed here, provide the means of aiding his intended political transformation of society via the privatization of religion. Spinoza reinterprets the supernatural spirit as the natural human mind; he discredits the idea of a people chosen by God; he eliminates religious ritual and transfers ceremonial authority to the state; he renarrates the work of God as the work of nature; and he views the Hebrew state as destined for failure. Biblical Psalms in the *Tractatus theologico-politicus* thus serve as one among many theo-political weapons Spinoza employs against his adversaries.

In the next chapter we take a look at the work of Fr. Richard Simon, one of Spinoza's contemporaries. Often it is asserted that Simon's work represents a more faithful alternative to Spinoza's. I argue, however, that Simon basically took Spinoza's work further in an even more skeptical direction. I then contrast Simon's historical-critical work with the earlier thought of St. Thomas More. More's work is useful because, although he did not engage in exegetical work recognizable as historical-critical, he did write in defense of textual criticism, philology, and history in biblical interpretation. More's defense of these disciplines might point a way forward in contemporary debates concerning theological exegesis.

43. Ibid., 222.

Table 1: Spinoza's Citations from the Pentateuch

Pentateuch Book	Number of Times Cited in Main Text	Number of Times Cited in Spinoza's Marginal Annotations
Genesis	38	6
Exodus	50	1
Leviticus	7	0
Numbers	18	6
Deuteronomy	83	1

Table 2: Spinoza's Citations from the Historical Books of the Old Testament

Historical Books	Number of Times Cited in Main Text	Number of Times Cited in Spinoza's Marginal Annotations
Joshua	22	1
Judges	20	1
Ruth	4	2
1 Samuel	25	2
2 Samuel	8	4
1 Kings	14	2
2 Kings	14	5
1 Chronicles	13	8
2 Chronicles	13	1
Ezra	14	5
Nehemiah	15	9
Esther	7	0

Table 3: Spinoza's Citations from the Wisdom Literature of the Old Testament

Wisdom Books	Number of Times Cited in Main Text	Number of Times Cited in Spinoza's Marginal Annotations
Job	11	0
Psalms	25	0
Proverbs	12	0
Ecclesiastes	7	0
Song of Songs	1	0

Table 4: Spinoza's Citations from the Major Prophets

Major Prophets	Number of Times Cites in Main Text	Number of Times Cited in Spinoza's Marginal Annotations
Isaiah	30	1
Jeremiah	39	1
Lamentations	1	0
Ezekiel	23	0
Daniel	14	1

Table 5: Spinoza's Citations from the Minor Prophets

Minor Prophets	Number of Times Cited in Main Text	Number of Times Cited in Spinoza's Marginal Annotations
Hosea	3	0
Joel	1	0
Amos	4	0
Obadiah	3	0
Jonah	6	0
Micah	2	0
Nahum	1	0
Zephaniah	2	0
Haggai	1	0
Zechariah	4	0
Malachi	3	0

Table 6: Spinoza's Citations from the Deuterocanon[44]

Deuterocanonical Text	Number of Times Cited in Main Text	Number of Times Cited in Spinoza's Marginal Annotations
Baruch	1	0
1 Maccabees	1	0

44. Although 1 Maccabees was not part of the Jewish biblical canon of Spinoza's contemporary Dutch Jews, nor was it a part of the Protestant canons of many of his Protestant interlocutors, he appears to use it as part of the Old Testament, as do Catholic and Orthodox Christians, as well as Ethiopian Jews. The same appears to be the case with Baruch, if he is in fact citing the Book of Baruch. In the case of 1 Maccabees, he cites it alongside Nehemiah, as if it is another Old Testament books. See Spinoza, *Theological-Political Treatise*, 149.

Table 7: Spinoza's Citations from the New Testament Gospels and Acts

Gospels	Number of Times Cited in Main Text	Number of Times Cited in Spinoza's Marginal Annotations
Matthew	14	1
Mark	0	1
John	2	0
Acts	1	0

Table 8: Spinoza's Citations from the Letters of St. Paul[45]

Letters of St. Paul	Number of Times Cited in Main Text	Number of Times Cited in Spinoza's Marginal Annotations
Romans	30	2
1 Corinthians	12	0
2 Corinthians	1	0
Galatians	3	0
Hebrews	2	0
1 Timothy	1	0
2 Timothy	1	0
Philemon	1	0

Table 9: Spinoza's Citations from the New Testament Catholic Epistles

Catholic Epistles	Number of Times Cited in Main Text	Number of Times Cited in Spinoza's Marginal Annotations
James	4	0
2 Peter	1	0
1 John	5	0
Jude	1	0

45. Included here are the New Testament letters traditionally attributed to St. Paul, including Hebrews.

Table 10: Spinoza's Citations from Early Jewish Sources

Early Jewish Sources	Number of Times Cited in Main Text	Number of Times Cited in Marginal Annotations
Philo	2	0
4 Ezra	1	0
Josephus	7	1

Table 11: Spinoza's Citations of Rabbinic, Medieval, and Later Jewish Sources

Rabbinic, Medieval, and Later Jewish Sources	Number of Times Cited in Main Text	Number of Times Cited in Spinoza's Marginal Annotations
Ibn Ezra	15	2
Maimonides	14	1
Talmud	8	0
Al–Fakhar	7	0
Rashi	3	1
Targum Jonathan	2	0
Joseph ben Shem Tov	1	0
Gersonides	0	1
David Kimchi	0	1
Abraham ben David	0	1

Table 12: Spinoza's Citations from Classical Sources

Classical Sources	Number of Times Cited in Main Text	Number of Times Cited in Spinoza's Marginal Annotations
Curtius	8	0
Tacitus	3	1
Seneca	2	0
Euclid	1	1
Aristotle	1	0
Ovid	1	0
Virgil	0	1

Table 13: Spinoza's Citations from his Contemporaries

Contemporaries	Number of Time Cited in Main Text	Number of Times Cited in Spinoza's Marginal Annotations
Spinoza (not by name, but text)	0	1
Hobbes	0	1
Lodewijk Meyer	0	3

Table 14: Spinoza's Citations from Other Sources

Other Sources	Number of Times Cited in Main Text	Number of Times Cited in Spinoza's Marginal Annotations
Ariosto	1	0
Qur'an	1	0
Bomberg's Edition of Bible	1	0
Tremellius's translation of the New Testament	0	1

Table 15: Spinoza's Use of the Word "Spirit"
(*ruach* **in Hebrew,** *spiritus* **in Latin**)[46]

Use of "Spirit" (*ruach* or *spiritus*)	Number of Occurrences
Total use of *ruach* or *spiritus*	148
Use of *ruach* in Hebrew font	57
Use of *ruach* transliterated using Latin letters	5

46. All of the data used in this article for Spinoza's use of "spirit" is based on his Latin text. The available modern translations have a tendency to use the term "spirit" (or the various modern language, e.g., French, equivalents) in places that Spinoza does not use it, as translations of other Latin words because the various translators think that it is the most appropriate translation, but are not relevant for Spinoza's discussion of "spirit" (*ruach*, *spiritus*). In addition, the modern translations have a tendency to omit using Hebrew font and solely include transliterations where applicable or just a translation into the modern language in which they are translating Spinoza. Spinoza, in contrast, occasionally transliterates the Hebrew after first including the word in Hebrew font, and will also often include the Old Testament quotation in Hebrew font followed by a Latin translation. Additionally, the total number of uses of *ruach* or *spiritus* accounts only for the occurrences where Spinoza uses the term "spirit" in reference to the "Spirit of God" or the "Holy Spirit," or as part of his linguistic study on the term.

Use of "Spirit" (*ruach* or *spiritus*)	Number of Occurrences
Use of *spiritus* as a Latin translation of the Hebrew *ruach*	50
"Spirit of God" as a complete phrase	17
"Holy Spirit" as a complete phrase	15
"spirit" as a stand–alone word and undefined	4
Uses of "spirit" (either *ruach* or *spiritus*) where Spinoza explicitly defines what it means	63
Use of "spirit of God" in reference to the prophets	4
"spirit of God" unmodified and undefined	7
"spirit" as a word to be defined	4
"spirit [*spiritus*] of God" as a translation of the Greek NT word *pneuma*, from a quotation	2
ruach in Hebrew font, as a Hebrew word whose meaning is at question	3
ruach transliterated as a Hebrew word whose meaning is at question	3
"spirit" as a translation of *ruach*, implying supernatural spirit, against which Spinoza will argue	1
ruach in Hebrew font as part of an OT quotation	38
"spirit" (*spiritus*) as a Latin translation of an OT quotation	36
ruach in Hebrew font as part of a Hebrew phrase not explicitly attached to a specific biblical verse	15
"spirit" (*spiritus*) as a Latin translation of a Hebrew phrase not explicitly attached to a specific biblical verse	15
"spirits" plural	1

Table 16: Spinoza's Definitions of "Spirit"
(*ruach* in Hebrew, *spiritus* in Latin)[47]

Meaning of "Spirit"	Number of Occurrences
spirit	1
wind	2

47. The English translations here are taken from Spinoza, *Theological-Political Treatise*. I certain places I will link them or modify them and place the Latin original in parentheses for purposes of clarification. In the first instance when he uses "spirit," for a single instance, it is the supernatural translation, which he notes is the normal way the word is translated in the Bible, but which he does not use in his work.

Meaning of "Spirit"	Number of Occurrences
breath	3
life	2
breathing/respiration	1
courage	1
strength (*viribus*), force (*vim, vi*), power (*vis, potentiam*)	4
ability	1
capacity	1
sentiment	1
mind	10
will	2
decision/decree	3
appetite/desire	5
movement of the mind	1
passion	3
talents	1
pride	1
humility	1
hatred	1
melancholy	2
kindness	2
virtue	3
soul	2
four quarters of the world	1
sides of anything that faces the four quarters of the world	1
heart	2
mercy	2
grace	1
healthy and happy mind	2

3

FAITH, REASON,
AND BIBLICAL INTERPRETATION

The Cases of Fr. Richard Simon
and St. Thomas More

THE DEBATE ABOUT THE role of faith, reason, and history in biblical interpretation is a long one that extends back into the medieval period. Contemporary concerns over an overly secularized historical exegesis often point to examples from the more skeptical seventeenth-century exegetes, like Hobbes and Spinoza. In the last chapter we took a closer look at Spinoza's exegesis, focusing on his use of the Psalms in his 1670 *Tractatus theologico-politicus*, situating that use within Spinoza's broader political context. Fr. Richard Simon is often put forward as a seventeenth-century alternative to Spinoza. Thus, in the first half of this chapter, I take a look at Simon, regarded as a first-rate historical biblical critic from historical criticism's earliest inception in the seventeenth century.

Simon could be presented as escaping the skepticism of the three more skeptical exegetes against whom he wrote in his own work, namely Isaac La Peyrère, Hobbes, and Spinoza, about whom I wrote in *Three Skeptics and the Bible*.[1] After all, Simon's historical critical work is a critique of the more perilous approaches of his three contemporaries, and Simon's exegesis is intended to be a robust defense of Catholic tradition. What I

---

1. See Morrow, *Three Skeptics and the Bible*, 54–84 on La Peyrère, 85–103 on Hobbes, and 104–38 on Spinoza.

hope to show in this chapter, however, is that Simon's apologetic is dubious at best, and his hermeneutic, although more learned and rigorous than even Spinoza's, is little more than an elaboration upon the very methods initiated by La Peyrère, Hobbes, and Spinoza. Far from being a defense of Catholic tradition, Simon's hermeneutic is a carefully crafted and subtle defense of Spinoza's exegetical method. Simon's method thus suffers from the same pitfalls as Spinoza's.

In the second half of this chapter, I then take a look at some of the theoretical work from the previous century at the dawn of the Reformation for an alternative approach to the question of the relationship between history and exegesis. In particular, I discuss St. Thomas More's Christian defenses of humanism and secular learning in relation to the study of Scripture. Several of More's letters, and his life in general, exemplify the possibility of maintaining the unity of faith and reason, as well as admitting both theology and history in biblical interpretation.

Richard Simon as a Father of Historical Criticism

Catholic scholars sometimes assume the path blazed by Simon is the best approach to questions of faith and history in exegesis. Hence this examination of Simon's work explores this possibility. What we find in the work of Simon, however, is not that far removed from what we find in La Peyrère, Hobbes, or Spinoza, even if the proposed intent contrasts with theirs. Although Simon argued against this triad, he followed their basic methodology, albeit to suit his own purposes.

Simon was born in 1638 in Dieppe, France, a mere ten years before the end of the Thirty Years' War.[2] He gained international fame through the publication of his masterpiece of historical criticism of the Old Testament, his 1678 *Histoire critique du Vieux Testament*.[3] As Hume proverbially woke Kant from his philosophical slumber, so Spinoza, it would seem, roused Simon to produce his own historical critical work.[4]

One of the main motives of Simon's *Histoire critique du Vieux Testament* differed greatly from the motives of his contemporaries: Simon was

2. For biographical information on Simon and on his biblical scholarship see Müller, *Richard Simon*; Müller, *Kritik und Theologie*; Nichols, "Richard Simon," 115–68; and Reventlow, "Richard Simon," 11–36.

3. Simon, *Histoire critique du Vieux Testament*. In this chapter all citations will be taken from this edition.

4. Ibid., author's preface, 76–78. See comments in Woodbridge, "Richard Simon's Reaction," 201–26.

attempting, in part, to provide a Catholic apologetic to defend the necessity of Catholic tradition vis-à-vis Protestant interlocutors who assumed a *sola Scriptura* position.[5] Indeed, his comments about the challenges posed by "the uncertainty of Hebrew grammar," and the like, resemble many of Spinoza's comments—but to a very different end.[6] Whereas Spinoza's project was to sound the death knell to theological exegesis, Simon instead emphasized the necessity of Catholic tradition. So threatening did Protestant theologians find his work that most of the published refutations of Simon for the next century were from Protestant intellectuals, not from Catholics.[7] As Manlio Iofrida remarks:

> In the end, then, chance, disorder consume the written text, reducing it to a kind of ruin. The philologist can undertake the task of restoration, but in the field of doctrine only the Church can guarantee the essential function, both religious and political, of the Sacred Scriptures. In this way, these Scriptures regress from an inspired corpus to something much less sacred, and are as a matter of fact secularized and stripped of sacredness. Imperfect, often incomprehensible, they assume the chiaroscuro of a historical document to be deciphered.[8]

Although Simon ostensibly provided a robust defense of Catholic tradition, and, by virtually all accounts, demolished any tenable notion of *sola Scriptura*, Scott Hahn and Benjamin Wiker make the observation that Simon's work provided little reason to rely on Catholic tradition at all, and, in fact, implicitly contributed to challenges opposing the authority of Catholic tradition. They note how, for Simon, "*traditio* acted more like an arbitrary Hobbesian authority settling intractable disputes than a divinely guided shepherd leading its flock into the deeper mysteries of God's Word . . . undermining the certainty of Scripture, Simon was also destroying *traditio*'s support of its authority and mission as affirmed from Scripture."[9]

---

5. Müller, "Grammatik und Wahrheit," 523; Gibert, *L'invention critique*, 177–78 and 198; Fleyfel, "Richard Simon," 473–74; and Stroumsa, "Richard Simon," 104.

6. Compare comments in Spinoza, *Tractatus theologico-politicus*, 7.12 and 14 with Simon, *Histoire critique du Vieux Testament*, author's preface, 81. All citations to the Latin text of Spinoza's *Tractatus theologico-politicus* will be taken from Spinoza, *Tractatus Theologico-Politicus*.

7. Shelford, "Of Sceptres and Censors," 177; and Nahkola, *Double Narratives*, 91–92.

8. Iofrida, "Original Lost," 215.

9. Hahn and Wiker, *Politicizing the Bible*, 399.

Simon thus set the stage for the more robust critique of Catholic tradition that would emerge among radical enlightenment thinkers.[10]

Simon was well versed in the arguments of his contemporaries. Whereas Simon had read the work of Hobbes and Spinoza, Simon not only read La Peyrère's work, but in fact knew him personally; La Peyrère and Simon became friends after La Peyrère's conversion to Catholicism and entrance into the Oratorians as a lay member. Prior to being expelled from the Oratorians, Simon served as an Oratorian priest.[11]

Simon's biblical method was thorough.[12] Simon maintained that several points needed to be followed in order to come to a proper understanding of the OT: (1) a good Hebrew text must be established;[13] (2) the Scriptures must be read critically as other books;[14] (3) the texts, including the variants in the diverse manuscript tradition being translated marginally, must be translated;[15] (4) finally, and perhaps most significantly, Simon provided a sort of *Forschungsgeschichte* (history of research), showing how earlier biblical interpreters dealt with the many historical problems in Scripture,[16] encouraging future biblical exegetes to follow the same path. Within this and prior sections, Simon himself basically followed the specific critical hermeneutic Spinoza articulated in the seventh chapter of his *Tractatus theologico-politicus*, but multiplying the problems encountered in such an investigation, far more thoroughly than Spinoza had.[17] As with Spinoza, Simon explicitly mentioned that the method he developed set up an "impossible" task (e.g., "to make a good translation of Scripture").[18] More than halfway through his mammoth tome, Simon conceded, "It even seems impossible to be able to succeed if we reflect on all the difficulties

10. Schwarzbach, "La fortune de Richard Simon," 225–39.

11. Pietsch, *Isaac La Peyrère*, 61 and 65; and Popkin, *Isaac La Peyrère*, 2–3, 9, 18–21, 49, 87–88, and 105.

12. Bernier, *La critique du Pentateuque*, 80–86; Knight, *Rediscovering the Traditions*, 38–42; and Woodbridge, "Richard Simon," 193–206.

13. Simon, *Histoire critique du Vieux Testament*, 3.1, 543–545; and Ska, "Richard Simon," 310–12.

14. Simon, *Histoire critique du Vieux Testament*, 3.1, 545. See also, e.g., the comment in Hazard, *La crise de la conscience*, 127, "If it is the Iliad, the Aeneid, or the Pentateuch, the principles of criticism are the same."

15. Simon, *Histoire critique du Vieux Testament*, 3.1, 545.

16. Ibid., 3.5–24.

17. See, especially Barthélemy, *Studies in the Text*, 60–62; Mirri, *Richard Simon*, 29–84; and Auvray, "Richard Simon et Spinoza," 211.

18. Simon, *Histoire critique du Vieux Testament*, 1.3, 119.

that have been noted above."[19] Yet, Simon maintained that the method must be employed, and an attempt at making a good translation must continue, to which end he himself labored hard.[20] In the end, with his *Histoire critique du Vieux Testament*, Simon "drowned his opponents in learning and in a sea of problems."[21]

Simon, like his friend La Peyrère, maintained that the Scriptures were copies of copies, whose present form was the work of various scribes.[22] Simon posited numerous unknown editors and compilers behind the Old Testament, attributing the redaction to court writers on behalf of the Hebrew state.[23] This did not pose a problem regarding the doctrine of inspiration, since Simon maintained that these editors and compilers were inspired by God. Of course, as scholars note, Simon's view of inspiration went hand-in-hand with the presence of all manner of distortions, errors, contradictions, and other infelicities in the biblical texts.[24] In the end, however, because of the nature of this layered editorial process, Scripture "was ultimately shrouded in darkness (not mystery), and only a historical-critical recovery of the original sources, an historical analysis of the needs and beliefs of the editor's own time, and finally, a psychological reconstruction of each editor could shed any light."[25] It was his overall denial of Mosaic authorship that got Simon in trouble, even though Simon conceded more of a role for Moses than even Hobbes had, not to mention Spinoza or La Peyrère.[26] In this context, Hahn and Wiker point out that:

> It was not simply the denial of Mosaic authorship, but his rejection of the *traditio's* attempt to explain the alleged textual imperfections by other means. As it developed, the Catholic position in regard to Scripture's seeming imperfections was that, what seemed disunited and imperfect, proved upon humble, faithful, and prayerful reading—guided by the Holy Spirit and Tradition—to be whole and harmonious, containing hidden perfections under seeming imperfections. Various ways arose to explain apparent imperfections: exegetes had recourse to a complex account of divine accommodation, to literal and

19. Ibid., 3.1, 543.

20. Reventlow, *History of Biblical Interpretation 4*, 85.

21. Popkin, "Bible Criticism and Social Science," 349.

22. Barthélemy, *Studies in the Text*, 75.

23. Bernier, "Richard Simon," 157–76.

24. Manuel, *Broken Staff*, 136; and McKane, *Selected Christian Hebraists*, 124.

25. Hahn and Wiker, *Politicizing the Bible*, 407.

26. Gibert, introduction, 35–37; and Steinmann, *Richard Simon*, 124–30.

spiritual senses, and even to the notion of purposely–placed divine stumbling blocks in the text to trip up the prideful and draw the humble to closer examination. Against this, Simon accepted the surface incongruities at face value—even rejoiced in them—so that the need for tradition became absolute.[27]

In short, Simon's acceptance of Spinoza's method led also to his accepting the conclusions of that method which identified purported unsolvable problems in the scriptural text. Rather than clinging to "reason" as an excuse to undermine the authority of the text, however, Simon clung to "faith" hence inadvertently also undermining the authority of the text, which he acknowledged was unable to withstand the scientific examination of reason.

Simon's work was condemned in France, at the instigation of Bossuet, and copies of *Histoire critique du Vieux Testament* were rounded up and thrown on fires. Simon's *Histoire critique du Vieux Testament* was subsequently published in the Dutch Republic when publication in France became impossible.[28] Bossuet, author of the Gallican Articles, did not oppose Simon's Gallicanist position.[29] Rather, Bossuet was upset by Simon's criticism of the Mosaic authorship of the Pentateuch, as well as what Bossuet saw as *Histoire critique du Vieux Testament*'s threats to more traditional Catholic views concerning biblical inspiration and tradition. Bossuet's conflict with Simon did not curb the enormous effect Simon's *Histoire critique du Vieux Testament* and other writings would have. Despite the aforementioned censure, Simon's corpus of biblical scholarship exerted an incredible influence on eighteenth-century Enlightenment biblical criticism.

Simon's work was brought into the English biblical critical world via Deist biblical critics and through Locke, who owned multiple copies of *Histoire critique du Vieux Testament*, one in which he made marginal annotations.[30] Simon's work also took Germany by storm, especially through the

27. Hahn and Wiker, *Politicizing the Bible*, 398.

28. Hazard, *La crise de la conscience*, 140; and Shelford, "Of Sceptres and Censors," 175. In a footnote, Shelford claims that, "At Bossuet's request, there were meetings between Simon and Pirot to develop a publishable version, but these efforts foundered when Simon walked out. Motivated by the possible repercussions of the seizure of an approved work, [Jean–Baptiste] Colbert [royal chancellor and thus royal censor] ordered another examination of *L'histoire critique* [sic]; once again, Simon refused to make the adjustments that were demanded" (175n62).

29. Perreau-Saussine, "Why Draw a Politics," 90–104.

30. Champion, "Père Richard Simon," 39–61.

work of the important Bible scholar Johann Salomo Semler.[31] In the end, we may conclude with Hahn and Wiker that, "Simon's attempt to vanquish Protestantism's claim of *sola scriptura* by amplifying Spinoza's approach to exegesis only served to provide a much firmer scholarly foundation for Spinozism."[32] Far from representing a different path from La Peyrère, Hobbes, and Spinoza, Simon's work became the vehicle for spreading the core principles of their biblical criticism through the Enlightenment and into the modern period. What is more, Simon's incredible erudition made their hermeneutic all the more formidable.

"Buried and Hard-to-Reach Treasure": St. Thomas More and the Unity of Faith and Reason

For a response to the type of criticism represented by Simon, and thus by La Peyrère, Hobbes, and Spinoza, I want to turn to the previous century, to the thought of St. Thomas More. More was not a Bible scholar, but he certainly engaged Scripture, and in fact many of his works provide an insight into his own exegesis which combined the best of traditional Christian exegesis with the tools of Renaissance humanism.[33] He argued passionately for reason, and chided clerics unwilling to use history and philology in an attempt to arrive at a more accurate text of the Bible, better translations, etc. Unlike the figures we have already discussed who would emerge on the scene in the next century, More was just as passionate about the necessity of faith as he was of reason. Faith and reason were inextricably bound in More's thought. In this, More's work reflected the holistic approach akin to that later articulated in the First Vatican Council's decree *Dei Filius* as well as in other magisterial documents such as Pope St. John Paul II's penultimate papal encyclical, *Fides et Ratio* and Pope Emeritus Benedict XVI's post-synodal apostolic exhortation, *Verbum Domini*.

---

31. Gibert, *L'invention critique*, 317–22; and Woodbridge, "German Responses," 65–87.

32. Hahn and Wiker, *Politicizing the Bible*, 423.

33. Rodgers, "Lessons of Gethsemane," 243–51; Marc'hadour, "Scripture in the Dialogue," 494–526; Marc'hadour, *Bible in the Works* 1; Marc'hadour, *Bible in the Works* 2; Marc'hadour, *Bible in the Works* 3; Marc'hadour, *Bible in the Works* 4; Marc'hadour, *Bible in the Works* 5; and Marc'hadour, *Thomas More et la Bible*.

More was born in London in 1477.[34] The son of a lawyer, More spent two years as a page to Archbishop John Morton, England's Lord Chancellor. At Oxford More thoroughly immersed himself in classical studies and he quickly became one of Europe's most prominent humanist scholars, producing works that epitomized that humanist tradition, including many translations and works on humanistic learning.[35] For a few years, apparently discerning whether or not he had a vocation to the religious life, More lived alongside the Carthusian monastery in London, actively participating in the Carthusian communal life of prayer.[36] He then became a lawyer, and was quite successful, carrying a reputation for professionalism and honesty wherever he went. He was elected to parliament, and then became the undersheriff of London, a post in which he served for about eight years, requiring him to provide legal advice to London's sheriff and mayor as well as serving as a judge.

In 1518, at the age of forty-one and after intentionally seeking to avoid official royal positions, More entered King Henry VIII's service as one of the King's counselors and became the King's secretary. He continued to advance in the King's service, and was awarded positions of increasing prestige on account of his tact, fidelity, and prudence. Significantly, More was instrumental in orchestrating the Peace of Cambrai which ended England's violent war with France. That same year (1529), at the age of fifty-one, King Henry VIII appointed More the Lord Chancellor, the first layman in history to hold such a position, a position exclusively followed by laymen.

The rest of the story is well known. More did his best to retain both his fidelity to the Church and to the King, but eventually was tried and found guilty, in spite of his courageous testimony, and despite the lack of credible evidence. On the last day of the octave of Easter, Sunday April 12, 1534 More was summoned for an investigation to take place on the following day. This would be the last day that More could roam about

---

34. For biographical information on More see especially Barron, "Making of a London Citizen," 3–21; McConica, "Thomas More," 22–45; Curtis, "More's Public Life," 69–92; Marshall, "Last Years," 116–38; and Ackroyd, *Life of Thomas More*.

35. On More's humanistic education and work, see, e.g., McConica, "Thomas More," 22–25; McCutcheon, "More's Rhetoric," 46–68; Curtis, "More's Public Life," 69–92; Kinney, introduction, xvii–xcii; Kristeller, "Thomas More," 5–22; Camporeale, "Da Lorenzo Valla," 9–102; Hexter, "Introduction," xlv–cv; and Surtz, "Introduction," clvi–clxxix.

36. On his time with the Carthusians, and especially on his spiritual formation, see the discussion in Vázquez de Prada, *Sir Tomás Moro*, 70–90; Ackroyd, *Life of Thomas More*, 96–111; and Wegemer, *Thomas More*, 10–17.

England as a free man, since he was imprisoned immediately following the royal inquiry. After the royal summons, More went home, "said goodnight to his family, went to church early the next morning, made his confession, heard Mass, and went to Communion."[37] He suffered immensely during his long imprisonment of 445 days, and after a sham trial More was executed by simple beheading.

What is often passed over was the heroic courage More showed at his trial, since the death he thought he was facing—as they read it out to him—was the same horrific procedure inflicted upon the Carthusians who broke their silence to speak the truth to the King. More's daughter Margaret was visiting him in his cell as the Carthusians were marched past on their way to their execution, and More would have been able to hear the gruesome torture and execution from within. We have a graphic description of their execution from four days later:

> After being dragged to the gallows, they made the condemned men climb one by one onto a cart that was then pulled away from under their feet, leaving them dangling in the air. They then immediately cut the rope, put them in a place prepared for the purpose, and, while they were still standing, cut off their private parts, which were thrown into the fire. Then they cut open their stomachs and ripped out their entrails; finally, they were decapitated and their bodies quartered before their hearts were removed and their mouths and faces wiped with them.[38]

This is what More expected to be his fate when he finally spoke out. King Henry commuted his sentence to simple beheading only on the very day More was escorted to the gallows.[39]

The few scholars aware of pre-nineteenth century and pre-Enlightenment roots of modern biblical criticism, who recognize prior influences as in the Renaissance turn *ad fontes*, to the sources, often identify Erasmus and More as important figures leading to the Protestant Reformation itself, and to the rise of the historical critical method of biblical studies,

---

37. Berglar, *Thomas More*, 170.

38. Ibid., 195.

39. For accounts of his imprisonment, trial, and execution, see especially, Kelly, Karlin, and Wegemer, preface, xi–xvii; Kelly, "Procedural Review," 1–52; Helmholz, "Natural Law," 53–70; Karlin and Oakley, "Guide to Thomas More's Trial," 71–93; McCutcheon, "Thomas More's Three Prison Letters," 94–110; Tugendhat, "Judicial Commentary," 111–19; Karlin, Jones, Fitzwater, Latta, Tugendhat, Kelly, Oakley, and House, "Judicial Commentary," 119–35; and Marshall, "Last Years," 116–38.

particularly as exemplified by such early critics as Simon.[40] This view should be nuanced, especially given that both More and Erasmus saw Luther and the Reformation as dangerous and as leading to war.

But even aside from that more blatant rejection of the Reformation as problematic, one crucial difference in approach, as contrasted with that of the Protestant reformers, is that More's and Erasmus's reforming influence always placed an emphasis on the development of virtue. For More, virtue allows reason to flourish, and only when both virtue and reason flourish can there exist a modicum of peace and justice. In the words of Gerard Wegemer, "When, therefore, Luther emphasized the corruption of reason, denied the possibility of achieving virtue, rejected free will, and taught that his elect had a nonrational access to truth, More and Erasmus strongly opposed these revolutionary views as both untrue and destructive. These revolutionary dogmas, they were convinced, could only lead to war and bloodshed."[41]

Contrary to the opinion of some scholars, More persisted in his defense and belief in humanism, albeit a humanism firmly set within a Christian, and indeed, a Catholic milieu.[42] For More, as became especially clear in his writings against Protestants, there always remained the need for an authority to interpret Scripture. There could be only anarchy with the embrace of a solipsistic assumption like *sola Scriptura*.[43] As Eamon Duffy explains, in More's way of thinking:

> The Bible can only be properly understood in the light of the Church's credo and its divinely inspired exegetical tradition, as embodied in the writings of "the olde holy fathers." The hermeneutic of suspicion, that systematic "dyffydens and mistrust" which More thought characterized the exegesis of Lutherans like Tyndale, caused them to set Bible and Church over against each other.[44]

This provides the necessary context for understanding More's thoughts on the role of such humanism, and especially philology and textual criticism, in theology and exegesis.

---

40. Duffy, "Common Knowen Multytude," 203–4; Gillespie, *Theological Origins of Modernity*, 92–100; and Shuger, *Renaissance Bible*, 16–18 and 22–24.

41. Wegemer, *Thomas More*, 97.

42. Duffy, "Common Knowen Multytude," 204–7 and 212.

43. Rex, "Thomas More and the Heretics," 97 and 100.

44. Duffy, "Common Knowen Multytude," 197.

Through his friendship with Erasmus, and the latter's Greek edition of the New Testament, More felt compelled to enter the fray when his humanist compatriot was being attacked by fellow Catholics, especially religious, over what they saw as philology's and secular learning's threat to the Catholic faith. More's responses indicate that he intended no harm to the Catholic faith, but rather that such fideistic complaints, as those which were leveled at Erasmus, were themselves deleterious. More saw the pursuit of textual criticism and the attempt at recovering the original wording of the Bible to be an important task that should be carried out to the best of the scholars's abilities. More regarded the tools of philology and textual scholarship, honed in the Renaissance, to be essential propaedeutics for theology. As with Erasmus, More was highly critical of much of what took place in the Schools, among scholastic theologians, but, as has been noted above, both were influenced by St. Thomas Aquinas and held the Angelic Doctor in very high esteem; Aquinas always escaped their liberally applied scathing criticisms.[45]

More never shied away from putting the best of secular learning at the service of faith. Perhaps the most important of More's defenses of such secular learning are in his letters in defense of Erasmus and of the study of Greek at the university: Letter to Martin Dorp (1515);[46] Letter to the University of Oxford;[47] Letter to Edward Lee (1519);[48] and Letter to a Monk (1519).[49] These letters can be much misunderstood, a possibility of which More seemed aware. More made clear throughout his Letter to a Monk, for example, that he was not attacking the religious state nor monasticism, but rather was calling his addressee to live out his state virtuously.[50]

45. Kinney, introduction, lxxii–xcii, especially lxxviii and lxxviii–lxxixn6; and Morales, "La formación espiritual," 439–89.

46. Latin text with English translation on opposing pages in Kinney, ed., *Complete Works of St. Thomas More 15*, 2–127.

47. LT and ET in ibid., 130–49.

48. LT and ET in ibid., 152–95.

49. LT and ET in ibid., 198–311.

50. E.g., consider More's statement to the monk in question: "among many of you, the more exclusively something is yours, the more value you place on it. For this reason many prize their own ceremonies more than those of their religious house, their own house's ceremonies more than those of their order, and whatever is exclusive to their order more than everything that is common to all religious orders, while they prize all that pertains to the religious somewhat more than they do these lowly and humble concerns that are not only not private to them but are common to the whole Christian people, such as those plebeian virtues of faith, hope, charity, fear of God, humility, and others of similar character" (ibid., 281). More is not here condemning the religious state, but rather he is elevating the key Christian virtues that all Christians should strive

Indeed, as More stated, "the same soil produces both wholesome and noxious herbs."[51]

More did not change tenor when responding to the Protestant Reformers, or when he defended monasticism, the religious life, and traditional Catholic pious practices. Rather, as Peter Berglar points out, More "always defended whatever was in the greatest jeopardy."[52] From 1515 to 1519, More thought that the value of secular learning for the faithful Christian was most in need of defense. By 1529 the climate had changed sufficiently that the religious state and monasticism itself was more in peril than philology, etc., and so More turned his apologetic to those battle fronts, defending the religious and monastic life to the hilt. Indeed, by 1540 not a single monastery, abbey, or the like, remained open in all of England. The crown had liquidated the monasteries, expelling and killing all of the religious who lived therein, their lands, their abbeys—after becoming state land, and thus giving birth to the phrase secularize in English idiom—passed into the hands of English nobles making them landed families.[53]

Erasmus's detractors were concerned for the future of the Church and the life of the faithful in light of the potential harm to which textual and philological studies like Erasmus's could lead. The path trodden by Protestant reformers like Luther validates this as a legitimate concern, as More must have realized once he had to address Protestantism. But the path Luther chose was not inevitable. The politics of the time—particularly the battle over the decaying remains of the medieval political order and the attempt to achieve territorial sovereignty excluding (foreign) papal control—and the ways in which the Latin Averroist tradition, nominalism, and Machiavellianism took root in England and Germany, had much to do with the successful violent transformation in Protestant lands.[54]

More (and Erasmus, for that matter) were not attempting to divorce philology completely from theology, unlike later scholars. More viewed

---

to exemplify, like the theological virtues of faith, hope, and love. The religious state, and monastic life, should be the settings where a religious, a monk, grows in such virtues. In the case More is discussing, in contrast, More accuses the monk of hiding vice behind a mere façade of virtue. For example, what is in fact defamation, an attack on one's reputation (in this case, against Erasmus), More states that the monk instead calls such defamation *fraterna monitio*, fraternal correction (ibid, 266, lines 13–14).

51. Ibid., 291.

52. Berglar, *Thomas More*, 134.

53. Duffy, *Stripping of the Altars*, 383–85, 397, 402–3, and 462.

54. Cavanaugh, *Myth of Religious Violence*, 156–77.

philology and other humanistic learning as essential tools in service of the faith. Such learning developed virtue, and provided, developed, and honed skills which would help sacred learning. Berglar identifies one root of More's vitriol in his Letter to a Monk as "the wrath of a layman in the face of monastic pride grounded in the belief that the monk in principle was the better Christian, the one closer to God and more sure of his salvation."[55] More's was not a simple angry reaction, however, but a *fraterna monitio* of sorts.[56] Whereas More accused the monk of defaming Erasmus's virtuous character under the guise of the praiseworthy practice of fraternal correction, More's response is in fact that which the monk claimed to have attempted: loving *fraterna monitio*. More argued that faith and reason must be united. Reason without faith is dead, but faith without reason is equally perilous.[57] In the end, for More, the Bible is "exceedingly difficult" to interpret. As he wrote, "Not one of the ancients, indeed, dared to claim that he understood it, for they thought that God, in his unfathomable wisdom, deliberately hid its meaning far from the surface precisely in order to challenge the sharpest eye and to stimulate minds with the promise of buried and hard–to–reach treasure which their very assurance might otherwise render indifferent to riches set plainly in view."[58] The textual, philological, and interpretive task then was regarded as a sacred work, a work of God.

More's theoretical comments on the relationship between faith and reason, Scripture and the Church's tradition and Magisterium, theology and philology, etc., were never divorced from the ultimate goal of virtue,

55. Berglar, *Thomas More*, 124.

56. See Kinney, *Complete Works of St. Thomas More 15*, 266.

57. More provides a concrete example of the centrality of uniting faith and reason. He recounts the incident, in which he took part, where a friar was teaching the laity that if they practiced a specific devotion to the Blessed Virgin they would be guaranteed salvation no matter what. When pushed to comment, More responded with, "first of all, nothing he had said in that entire sermon would seem really persuasive to anyone who did not accept the miracles that he had reported, a response which would not necessarily contravene Christian faith, and that even if those miracles were true they were hardly an adequate basis for the thesis at hand. For while you might easily find a prince who would sometimes pardon even his enemies at his mother's entreaty, no prince anywhere is foolish enough to promulgate a law which would encourage his own subjects to defy him by promising immunity to every traitor who propitiated his mother with a set form of flattery" (Kinney, ed., *Complete Works of St. Thomas More 15*, 289). See ibid, 284–91 for the recounting of the entire incident. More makes clear that he is not disparaging the cult of the Blessed Virgin which he explicitly labels "a most wholesome devotion" (ibid., 291), but rather is just disparaging an abuse which abdicates reason. Such faith alone is not faith at all, but is more akin to superstition.

58. From his Letter to Martin Dorp, in ibid., 59.

sanctity, divinization, and union with God. This can be seen in the unified spiritual and material fabric of More's entire life, as Berglar makes clear:

> Conscience did not allow More to wait idly for death and the hereafter, but spurred him on to prepare for it. That meant seeking and following Christ, which for him meant loving his neighbor in everyday life by conscientiously fulfilling his professional duties, goodness in family life, work that strives to achieve the physical, intellectual, and spiritual welfare of one's neighbor. And something more: living at close quarters with Jesus Christ in prayer, Holy Mass, the sacraments, and sacrifice. This unity of Christian life was ingrained in him—a cheerful dinner companion who was also a deep thinker, an intellectual polemicist and valued jurist who was a humble man of prayer and preferred mercy to strict justice, a generous and practical family man who yearned for the stillness of a cloister. This servant of the King served the King of Kings at Mass; beneath the trappings of office, this courtier wore a penitent's garment that caused sores; this successful literate man offset the favor of his sovereign and popularity with the public by fasting, going without sleep, and caring for the poor. For him, *memento mori* was never separate from *memento vivere*.[59]

Although More's life exemplified the universal call to holiness that would later come from *Lumen Gentium*'s fifth chapter at Vatican II, this was likely a concept More would have been unable to articulate. He lived the virtues in his ordinary family and work life to a heroic degree, but he was canonized for his heroic act of martyrdom. He always held religious life, particularly monastic life, and in a very special way, the Carthusians, in highest esteem. He viewed such religious life as an ideal he was unable to live, viewing his married life as an impediment, a necessary concession, on his path toward God.[60] And yet, one could argue that the sanctity he achieved in his ordinary life, lovingly embracing the little martyrdoms of each day, is what prepared him for courageously facing his execution. He lived a form of union with God, while deeply engaged in family, professional, and scholarly pursuits; immersed in the world, he was at the same time immersed in God. It is within this context that he placed his secular learning, which was always at the service of developing virtue. In this way,

59. Berglar, *Thomas More*, 17.

60. Kinney, introduction, lxxxviiin1; and Gordon, "Monastic Achievement," 199–214.

under the loving guidance of the Church, faith, and reason together were seen as able to elevate the soul to God.

Far too often, Catholic biblical studies in the academy proceeds along the lines of the work of Richard Simon, who in turn followed the earlier more skeptical work of La Peyrère, Hobbes, and Spinoza. The problem with such pursuits is not found in the admirable mastery of languages, philological and textual methodologies, engagement in rigorous and disciplined archaeological and other historical pursuits, but rather in the severing of the ties between exegesis and the magisterium, the science of criticism and the Church's tradition, philology and traditional Catholic biblical interpretation exemplified in patristic and medieval exegesis.

It should not be surprising that some historical scholars might consider the past events related to biblical interpretation in the seventeenth century and conclude that there was no other way to proceed other than the route marked out by La Peyrère, Hobbes, Spinoza, and Simon. To such scholars, the foundations of the historical critical method emerged solely from an attempt to embrace unadulterated reason and to apply a scientific method to a text that was a historical document as much as a canonical and ecclesiastical one. The conclusion of the historical narrative when presented in this particular way can only be emphatic support that accords hegemony to the approach begun by these individuals. My inclusion of More into this narrative, however, is a plea for a reconsideration of these foregone conclusions.

More's inextricable uniting of faith and reason in his defense of Christian humanism, added to Erasmus's extensive philological work in seeking to recover a more accurate and faithful understanding of the biblical text, indicates that there was another possibility for an interpretation of the Bible that would not pit reason against faith in the examination of the scriptural text. Here we have a scholarly Catholic in the sixteenth century who did not see a need to undermine the authority of the biblical text, or the magisterium, for that matter, in order to apply methods of reason, such as philology and history, to its interpretation. That this particular route, holding together faith and reason, was not shared by La Peyrère, Hobbes, Spinoza, and Simon may in fact be the best indication that their motives were primarily political, rather than strictly theological, well-intentioned hopes for a more rigorous interpretation.

For too long, it has been commonplace to accept the conclusions of these methods without ever considering the motivations behind the method which may affect the way they can be used. For this reason, Ratzinger implored Catholic exegetes in his provocative "Schriftsauslegung im Widerstreit," critically to examine the philosophical underpinnings of their exegesis, philosophies which often remain unexamined and yet even more frequently predetermine the results of such exegesis, or at least severely limit the range of possible results often to those antithetical to the faith.[61] As Benedict XVI wrote, "The wanting of a hermeneutic of faith in relation to Scripture not only entails the concept of absence; in its place another hermeneutic necessarily comes in, a positivist hermeneutic which favors the secular, ultimately based on the conviction that the Divine does not intervene in human history. . . . Such a position can only prove harmful to the life of the Church."[62] In contrast to this, More provides an example of how Catholic exegetes might approach the study of Sacred Scripture. It is an approach demonstrated by More's scholarship, his life, and his death. This saintly witness reflects what John Paul II would articulate over 450 years later, namely that, "faith purifies reason. As a theological virtue, faith liberates reason from presumption."[63]

In the next chapter we will see how biblical studies in the eighteenth century chose neither the path of Simon nor the path of More, and yet, biblical studies became an autonomous academic discipline in its own right, following the basic blueprint Spinoza laid down in the seventeenth century, which Spinoza bequeathed via Simon and via the many responses they both elicited. By and large the biblical studies which emerged in the eighteenth century severed ties with theology, but not for reasons primarily of skepticism or secularism. Rather, the Bible became an important means of the appropriation of civic virtues that could be gleaned from the ancient Hebraic past. The Bible would be made strange by being pushed into the ancient past as a historical document, and then could be mined for the purposes of culture and statecraft. This was not a skeptical attempt to deconstruct the Bible, but rather a means of creating a new autonomous discipline founded along the paradigm of classical studies, which could thrive at the newly formed and reconfigured Enlightenment universities. What would emerge would be the discipline recognizable as modern biblical studies. This can be seen no clearer than in the life and work of Johann

61. Ratzinger, *Schriftsauslegung im Widerstreit*, 15–44.

62. Benedict XVI, *Verbum Domini*, no. 35. English translation slightly modified from Vatican website.

63. John Paul II, *Fides et Ratio*, no. 76. English translation from Vatican website.

David Michaelis (1717 to 1791). So it is to Michaelis and the burgeoning of biblical studies at the University of Göttingen that we now turn.

4

BIBLICAL STUDIES AT THE
ENLIGHTENMENT UNIVERSITY

IN HIS COLLECTION OF essays, *The Hebrew Bible, the Old Testament, and Historical Criticism*, Jon Levenson remarked that, "historical criticism is the form of biblical studies that corresponds to the classical liberal political ideal. It is the realization of the Enlightenment project in the realm of biblical scholarship."[1] In the last chapter, we took a look at the pioneering work of Richard Simon (1638 to 1712) and I argued that, despite his claims to the contrary, Simon's work was very much a continuation of Spinoza's more skeptical approach. The sixteenth-century theoretical work of St. Thomas More provides a more faithful example of integrating faith and reason in biblical interpretation. In this chapter, I will discuss the shift that occurred in the eighteenth century, primarily represented in the work of Johann David Michaelis (1717 to 1791), within its social and historical context. In order to do this, I will primarily be following Michael Legaspi's important volume on Michaelis and the transformation of biblical studies at the University of Göttingen.[2]

Biblical scholars rarely concern themselves with the history of their discipline. In part this is because the discipline of modern biblical studies has for so long styled itself on the hard sciences, and participates in what Pascal termed *l'esprit géométrique*, the spirit of geometry whereby

1. Levenson, *Hebrew Bible*, 118.

2. Legaspi, *Death of Scripture*. This present chapter originated as a lengthy review of Legaspi's volume in Morrow, "Enlightenment University," 897–922.

mathematics serves as the paradigm for true rationality. John Barton explains well historical criticism's original ostensible intent; it "was meant to be value-neutral, or disinterested. It tried, so far as possible, to approach the text without prejudice, and to ask not what it meant 'for me', but simply what it meant."[3] In 1988, Pope Emeritus Benedict XVI—then Joseph Cardinal Ratzinger—delivered his now famous lecture, "Biblical Interpretation in Crisis," wherein he issued a clarion call for a *"Kritik der Kritik,"* a criticism of criticism; a self-criticism of historical critical methodology.[4] The debate about biblical exegesis, including the role of history and of theology in biblical interpretation, continued to be a major theme in Pope Benedict's thought.[5] Far from a lone voice, Benedict has been joined by a number of scholars—Jewish, Protestant, and Catholic—in his concern over the present status of biblical interpretation.

One important area of study, a field which needs many more laborers, is the history of biblical scholarship. Biblical scholarship should be encouraged to examine its own foundations, its own history, in part to understand better the philosophical and political influences which gave shape and texture to the methods which continue to be uncritically employed. Michael Legaspi's *The Death of Scripture and the Rise of Biblical Studies*, is a welcome contribution to this ongoing discussion, and his unique contribution focusing on Michaelis and Göttingen is the main reason I think expositing his work in this chapter is worthwhile.[6] The pressures and influences exerted on the discipline of biblical studies as it developed that have been most neglected in scholarly discussions involve those exerted by the modern state. Legaspi brings this to the fore of his discussion in nu-

---

3. Barton, *Old Testament*, 203.

4. Ratzinger, *Schriftauslegung im Widerstreit*, 22.

5. Ibid., 15–44; Ratzinger, "Kirchliches Lehramt," 522–29; Ratzinger, *Jesus of Nazareth I*, xi–xxiii; Ratzinger, *Verbum Domini*, nos. 29–41; and Ratzinger, *Jesus of Nazareth II*, xiv–xv. For important studies of Ratzinger's/Benedict's thoughts on modern biblical criticism see, e.g., Hahn, "Authority of Mystery," 97–140; Raurell, "Mètode d'aproximació," 435–58; Hahn, "At the School of Truth," 80–115; Hahn, "Hermeneutic of Faith," 415–40; and Hahn, *Covenant and Communion*, especially chapter 2, "The Critique of Criticism: Beginning the Search for a New Synthesis," 25–40, and chapter 3, "The Hermeneutic of Faith: Critical and Historical Foundations for a Biblical Theology," 41–62. When addressing the difficulties posed by the unrecognized philosophical presuppositions of modern biblical criticism, Ratzinger often brings up the example of Rudolf Bultmann. A number of important works situating Bultmann's hermeneutics in their broader intellectual/cultural/philosophical context have come out, e.g., Jonas, *Gnostic Religion*, 320–40; Blank, *Analyse und Kritik*; Waldstein, "Foundations of Bultmann's Work," 115–45; and Waldstein, "Analogia Verbi," 93–140.

6. Legaspi, *Death of Scripture*.

merous enlightening ways, as when he underscores the importance of the state-sponsored Enlightenment universities. Commenting on "the fate of theology" among German scholars in the nineteenth century, he explains:

> Striking a Faustian bargain with the growing power of the state, they maintained their religious and cultural inheritance by folding the authority of the Bible and of the Protestant theological tradition into the larger programs of *Verwissenschaftlichung* (scientization), *Entkonfessionalisierung* (deconfessionalization), *Professionalisierung* (professionalization), and *Verstaatlichung* (nationalization)—all programs centered at the university.[7]

Before moving further into Legaspi's history of biblical studies in the eighteenth century work of Michaelis at Göttingen, and its broader cultural and historical context, it is well worth surveying the history of the discipline of the history of biblical scholarship itself.

Overview of the History of Modern Biblical Scholarship

Over the past several decades, a number of important studies have been published highlighting the historical, political, theological, and philosophical contexts to the development of modern biblical criticism, from the medieval period to the twentieth century. Prior to the 1980s there had been some scholarship in this field, like Hans-Joachim Kraus' 1956 *Geschichte der historisch-kritischen Erforschung des Alten Testaments* and Hans Frei's 1974 *The Eclipse of the Biblical Narrative*.[8] It is especially after the end of the 1970s, however, that a scholarly focus on the history of modern biblical scholarship has grown to become a field in its own right.[9]

---

7. Ibid., 29.

8. Kraus, *Geschichte der historisch–kritischen*; and Frei, *Eclipse of the Biblical Narrative*. There were likewise a few specialized books that dealt with one or a few of the significant figures in this early history or with the scholarship of discreet biblical books, e.g., Zac, *Spinoza et l'interprétation*; Scholder, *Ursprunge und Probleme*; Gasque, *History of the Criticism*; and Fatio and Fraenkel, ed., *Histoire de l'exégèse*. Some early studies existed as well in the form of scholarly articles and book chapters, but these were very rare, e.g., Hazard, *La crise de la conscience*, 2nd part, chapter 3, "Richard Simon et l'exégèse biblique," 125–36; and Momigliano, "La nuova storia," 773–90.

9. A large amount of scholarship in this field was already building in the 1970s in the form of scholarly articles. One important example here is the work on Isaac La Peyrère and Baruch Spinoza published by Richard Popkin, within the history of philosophy, e.g., Popkin, "Bible Criticism and Social Science," 339–60; Popkin, "Development of Religious Scepticism," 271–80; and Popkin, "Spinoza and La Peyrère," 172–95. Similarly important works had also been published by Bible scholars, but these were

In 1980 Henning Graf Reventlow published *Bibelautorität und Geist der Moderne.*[10] Reventlow's groundbreaking work demonstrated the importance of sixteenth and seventeenth century England to the rise of modern biblical criticism. The idea that modern biblical criticism's roots can be traced to eighteenth or nineteenth century Germany remains the commonly received scholarly opinion. Reventlow's work, however, showed how Germany was a late-comer to modern biblical criticism; eighteenth-century German biblical criticism built upon the critical work of English biblical exegetes from the sixteenth, seventeenth, and eighteenth centuries.[11]

Although not primarily a work in the history of scholarship, mention should be made of the first installment in 1982 of the soon-to-be 5 -volume series, *Critique textuelle de l'Ancien Testament,* edited by Dominique Barthélemy.[12] *Critique textuelle de l'Ancien Testament* is the result of the Hebrew Old Testament Text Project Committee of the United Bible Societies which began in 1969, which has resulted in the new *Biblia Hebraica Quinta* editions of the Hebrew text of the Old Testament, which is in the process of replacing the *Biblia Hebraica Stuttgartensia.* The pur-

even rarer, e.g., Goshen-Gottstein, "Christianity," 69–88.

10. Reventlow, *Bibelautorität.*

11. The 1980s witnessed an incredibly rapid increase in scholarly literature, in the form of both books and articles, dealing with the history of modern biblical criticism in the early modern era, coming especially from historians of philosophy and Bible scholars interested in the history of their discipline. Examples include: Grafton, *Joseph Scaliger* 1; Goshen–Gottstein, "Textual Criticism," 365–99; Sarna, "Modern Study," 19–27; Katchen, *Christian Hebraists;* Laplanche, *L'écriture;* Goshen–Gottstein, "Foundations of Biblical Philology," 77–94; Popkin, *Isaac La Peyrère;* Osier, "L'herméneutique de Hobbes," 319–47; Berlin and Katchen, ed., *Christian Hebraism;* Goshen-Gottstein, "Revival of Hebraic Studies," 185–91; Iofrida, "Original Lost," 211–19; Pacchi, "Hobbes and Biblical Philology," 231–39; Sermoneta, "Biblical Anthropology," 241–47; Armogathe, ed., *Le Grand Siècle;* Yovel, *Spinoza and Other Heretics I;* and ibid., *Spinoza and Other Heretics II.* This decade also saw a number of important studies contextualizing later seventeenth-, eighteenth-, and nineteenth-century scholarship, e.g., Schwaiger, ed., *Historische Kritik;* Rendtorff, "Die Hebräische Bibel," 32–47; Momigliano, "Religious History," 49–64; Smend, "Julius Wellhausen and his *Prolegomena,*" 1–20; Knight, "Wellhausen," 21–36; Hayes, "Wellhausen," 37–60; Miller, "Wellhausen," 61–73; Silberman, "Wellhausen," 75–82; Childs, "Wellhausen," 83–88; Dahl, "Wellhausen," 89–110; Rudolph, "Wellhausen," 111–55; Belaval and Bourel, eds., *Le siècle des Lumières;* and Reventlow, Sparn, and Woodbridge, ed., *Historische Kritik.*

12. The volumes that have been published thus far include: Barthélemy, ed., *Critique textuelle* 1; Barthélemy, ed., *Critique textuelle* 2; Barthélemy, ed., *Critique textuelle* 3; and Barthélemy, ed., *Critique textuelle* 4; and Barthélemy, ed., *Critique textuelle* 5. I owe James Sanders, who served on the committee with Fr. Barthélemy, tremendous gratitude for making me aware of this supremely important multi-volume work.

pose of *Critique textuelle de l'Ancien Testament* is to serve as a text critical commentary on the Hebrew text of the Old Testament. Thus the focus is more on textual criticism than historical criticism. In the first volume, however, Fr. Barthélemy wrote an introduction spanning over 100 pages, roughly the first half of which he spent detailing the history of modern biblical scholarship, from the medieval period (including the important work of Judeo-Arabic exegesis) through the development of modern historical criticism, including a very good discussion of seventeenth century figures like Spinoza and Simon. Regretfully, *Critique textuelle de l'Ancien Testament* has been too little utilized by scholars, and Fr. Barthélemy's fine monograph-length essay has received even less attention.

John Rogerson's *Old Testament Criticism in the Nineteenth Century* was released in 1984.[13] Rogerson's important work, in a sense, picks up where Reventlow's earlier volume left off. Whereas Reventlow traced the early years of modern biblical criticism in England (especially among the Deists) to Germany, Rogerson focuses more on how biblical criticism then developed in Germany and how eventually German biblical criticism was then later received by England. In 1991, J. C. O'Neill published *The Bible's Authority*.[14] This was an important text walking through several significant figures within the history of biblical scholarship from the eighteenth to twentieth centuries. Most significantly, O'Neill placed these figures within their intellectual and historical contexts.

The following year, 1992, saw the publication of Hava Lazarus-Yafeh's tremendously important *Intertwined Worlds*.[15] Lazarus-Yafeh showed how influential medieval Muslim biblical criticism was on significant medieval Jewish and Christian exegetes, likely making its way into the modern period.[16] The same year Lazarus-Yafeh's work was published, Rogerson came out with his important study of one of the most significant early nineteenth

13. Rogerson, *Old Testament Criticism*.

14. O'Neill, *Bible's Authority*.

15. Lazarus-Yafeh, *Intertwined Worlds*. Some earlier scholarship exists which is in line with Lazarus-Yafeh's work, highlighting the importance of medieval Muslim biblical scholarship for what came later in the Renaissance, Reformation, and Enlightenment, e.g., Algermissen, "Die Pentateuchzitate Ibn Hazms,"; Arnaldez, "Spinoza," 151–74; Powers, "Reading/Misreading," 109–21; Adang, "Schriftvervalsing," 197–98; and Freedman, "Father of Modern Biblical Scholarship," 31–38.

16. She also published important articles that would be well worth reading for Bible scholars interested in the probable influence of medieval Muslim biblical criticism and philosophy on medieval Jewish and Christian biblical exegesis, which likely contributed to the rise of modern biblical criticism in western European universities. See, e.g., Adang, "*Taḥrīf*," 81–88; and Adang, "Some Neglected Aspects," 61–84.

century biblical critics, *W.M.L. de Wette: Founder of Modern Biblical Criticism*.[17] De Wette's work was foundational for nineteenth century historical criticism of the Old Testament, and particularly pentateuchal criticism. Rogerson's intellectual biography places de Wette in his broader social, political, and historical context. Also in 1992, William Baird published his *History of New Testament Research Vol. I*.[18] This volume placed many New Testament critics in their historical and intellectual contexts.

Another one of Rogerson's volumes on the history of modern biblical scholarship, *The Bible and Criticism in Victorian England*, was released on 1995, which highlighted William Robertson Smith's important place in bringing German biblical criticism back to the English speaking world, where, ironically, the seeds of German biblical criticism partially germinated a century-and-a-half earlier.[19] In 1999 David Dungan published *A History of the Synoptic Problem*.[20] Dungan's volume has proved controversial, but he includes a number of important chapters dealing with both ancient—e.g., Porphyry—and modern—e.g., Spinoza, Locke, Griesbach, and Holtzmann—figures who are significant within this broader history.

In 2001 Reventlow published his *Epochen der Bibelauslegung 4*.[21] In this fourth volume in Reventlow's impressive series on the history of biblical interpretation, Reventlow provides historical and biographical background to significant figures in early modern to contemporary biblical criticism, from the sixteenth to the twentieth centuries, including Thomas Hobbes (1588 to 1679), Baruch Spinoza (1632 to 1677), Richard Simon (1638 to 1712), Hermann Samuel Reimarus (1694 to 1768), Gotthold Ephraim Lessing (1729 to 1781), Johann Salomo Semler (1725 to 1791),

17. Rogerson, *W.M.L. de Wette*.

18. Baird, *History of New Testament Research I*.

19. Rogerson, *Bible and Criticism*.

20. Dungan, *History of the Synoptic Problem*. In the 1990s a flood of scholarly literature continued to expand the field of the history of modern biblical criticism, e.g., Kugel, "Bible in the University," 143–65; Grafton, *Defenders of the Text*, especially ch. 8, "Isaac La Peyrère and the Old Testament," 204–13; Gibert, *Petite histoire*; Grafton, *Joseph Scaliger 2*; Force and Popkin, ed., *Books of Nature*; Shuger, *Renaissance Bible*; Reventlow and Farmer, ed., *Biblical Studies*; Johnstone, ed., *William Robertson Smith*; Walther, "Biblische Hermeneutik," 227–99; Marchand, *Down from Olympus*; Burnett, *From Christian Hebraism*; Cooke, *Hobbes and Christianity*; Hornig, *Johann Salomo Semler*; Räisänen, *Marcion*, in particular, "The Bible and the Traditions of the Nations: Isaac La Peyrère as a Precursor of Biblical Criticism," 137–52; Stroumsa, "Jewish Myth," 19–35; Stroumsa, "Comparatisme et philologie," 47–62; Pasto, "Islam's 'Strange Secret Sharer,'" 437–74; Pasto, "When the End," 157–202; Champion, "Père Richard Simon," 39–61; and Tricaud, "L'Ancien Testament," 229–38.

21. Reventlow, *Epochen der Bibelauslegung 4*.

Johann Gottfried Eichhorn (1752 to 1827), Wilhelm Martin Leberecht de Wette (1780 to 1849), David Friedrich Strauss (1808 to 1874), Ferdinand Christian Baur (1792 to 1860), Heinrich Ewald (1803 to 1875), Julius Wellhausen (1844 to 1918), and Rudolf Bultmann (1884 to 1976). Unlike so many others, however, Reventlow examines and summarizes the major works of each scholar. Reventlow's work, without a doubt, remains one of the most important of its kind, even a decade later. In 2005, Jonathan Sheehan published *The Enlightenment Bible*.[22] Johann David Michaelis, who is the main focus of Legaspi's own work, plays an important part in Sheehan's story. Sheehan's text describes the ways in which the Enlightenment changed the way in which the Bible was viewed, from a primarily theological text, to a cultural-historical one which became foundational to the Western world.

In 2007, Rudolf Smend published his *From Astruc to Zimmerli*.[23] Unlike O'Neill's earlier work, Smend focuses exclusively on Old Testament scholarship. Smend's portraits of each figure are highly illuminating and would be a very useful introduction to their historical contexts. In 2008, Magne Sæbø published the edited volume, *Hebrew Bible/Old Testament: The History of Its Interpretation II*.[24] The third installment of this important series, Sæbø's work provides very good brief essays on relevant themes from the Old Testament scholarship from the Renaissance to the Enlightenment, as well as on particular exegetes, giving brief biographical accounts which help situate them in their proper historical contexts. Themes include: the idea of history in the Renaissance; Scholasticism and medieval theological education; the rise of universities in medieval Europe;

---

22. Sheehan, *Enlightenment Bible*.

23. Smend, *From Astruc*.

24. Sæbø, ed., *Hebrew Bible/Old Testament II*. The first decade of the twenty–first century saw an immense amount of scholarly literature develop within the history of modern biblical scholarship, e.g., Howard, *Religion and the Rise of Historicism*; Stroumsa, "Homeros Hebraios," 87–100; Preus, *Spinoza and the Irrelevance of Biblical Authority*; Arnold and Weisberg, "Centennial Review," 441–57; Gibert, *L'Invention de l'exégèse moderne*; Pasto, "W. M. L. de Wette," 33–52; Coudert, *Hebraica Veritas*; Müller, *Kritik und Theologie*; Coleman, "Thomas Hobbes," 642–69; Meeks, "Nazi New Testament Professor," 513–44; Arnold and Weisberg, "Delitzsch in Context," 37–45; Schönert and Vollhardt, ed., *Geschichte der Hermeneutik*; Van Seters, *Edited Bible*; Frampton, *Spinoza and the Rise of Historical Criticism*; Jarick, ed., *Sacred Conjectures*; Jindo, "Revisiting Kaufmann," 41–77; Reiser, *Bibelkritik und Auslegung*, for the purposes of our present discussion, especially chapter 7, "Richard Simons biblische Hermeneutik,"185–217, and chapter 8, "Die Prinzipien der biblischen Hermeneutik und ihr Wandel unter dem Einfluß der Aufklärung," 219–76; Jorink, "Horrible and Blasphemous," 429–550; Kratz, "Eyes and Spectacles," 381–402; and Machinist, "Road Not Taken," 469–531.

the quest for *Hebraica veritas*; Renaissance Jewish biblical scholarship; early modern Spanish biblical interpretation; polyglot Bibles; Waldensian, Lollard, and Hussite biblical interpretation; the Reformation in England and Scotland; biblical interpretation at the Councils of Constance, Florence, and Trent; Deism; Hasidism and biblical interpretation; the French Revolution; etc. Figures examined include: Nicholas of Lyra; Gersonides; Marsilio Ficino; Pico della Mirandola; Isaac Abarbanel; Erasmus; Reuchlin; Levita; Wyclif; Hus; Luther; Zwingli; Calvin; Bucer; Melanchthon; Cajetan; Bellarmine; a Lapide; Cappel; the Buxtorfs; Socinus; Grotius; La Peyrère; Descartes; Spinoza; Simon; Astruc; Toland; Reimarus; Lessing; Lowth; Geddes; Michaelis; Semler; Eichhorn; et al. Each entry includes very helpful select bibliographies.

More recently, in 2010 Pierre Gibert published *L'invention critique de la Bible*.[25] Gibert's important study focuses on the seventeenth century, and especially on the work of Spinoza and Richard Simon, but he also includes very important discussions of earlier work (e.g., Lorenzo Valla, Elias Levita, Erasmus, Luther, and Isaac La Peyrère) and later work (especially Astruc). Much of my own scholarly contributions have been devoted to this field as well, including the present volume.[26]

---

25. Gibert, *L'invention critique*. Of course I have left many studies out, and the examples I provide in the footnotes are far from exhaustive. There are a number of more popular treatments of the history of scholarship, as well, written by scholars, like Levenson, *Hebrew Bible*; and the first chapter, "The Rise of Modern Biblical Scholarship," in Kugel, *How to Read the Bible*, 1–46. In this context, mention should be made of the fine, albeit controversial, work of Harrisville and Sundberg, *Bible in Modern Culture*. Hahn and Wiker, *Politicizing the Bible*, represents the most important work in this area, a real milestone in the history of modern biblical scholarship, showing the important role numerous figures played in the rise of historical criticism, figures including Marsilius of Padua, William of Ockham, Wycliffe, Machiavelli, Luther, King Henry VIII, Descartes, Hobbes, Spinoza, Simon, Locke, and Toland—and situating each of these figures in their broader historical, political, philosophical, and theological contexts.

26. E.g., Morrow, "Acid of History,"; Morrow, "St. Thomas More,"; Morrow, "Spinoza,"; Morrow, "*Dei Verbum*,"; Morrow, "Fate of Catholic Biblical Interpretation,"; Morrow, "Loisy,"; Morrow, *Three Skeptics and the Bible*; Morrow, "Babylon in Paris," 261–76; Morrow, "Averroism, Nominalism, and Mechanization," 1293–1340; Morrow, "Faith, Reason and History," 658–73; Morrow, "Cut Off from Its Wellspring," 547–58; Morrow, "Spinoza's Use of the Psalms," 1–18; Morrow, "Secularization, Objectivity, and Enlightenment," 14–32; Morrow, "Alfred Loisy," 87–103; Morrow, "Untold History," 145–55; Morrow, "*Études Assyriologie*," 3–20; Morrow, "Alfred Loisy's Developmental Approach," 324–44; Morrow, "Enlightenment University," 897–922; Morrow, "Historical Criticism," 189–221; Morrow, "Babylonian Myths," 43–62; Morrow, "Pre–Adamites," 1–23; Morrow, "*Leviathan*," 33–54; Morrow, "French Apocalyptic Messianism," 203–13; Morrow, "Modernist Crisis," 265–80; Morrow, "Early Modern Political Context," 7–24; Morrow, "Politics of Biblical Interpretation," 528–45; and Morrow, "Bible in Captivity," 285–99.

The Decomposition of the Scriptural Bible and the Rise of the Academic Bible

The Death of Scripture and the Rise of Biblical Studies, which has been published as part of Oxford University Press's Oxford Studies in Historical Theology series, began as Legaspi's Harvard University PhD dissertation, entitled, "Reviving the Dead Letter: Johann David Michaelis and the Quest for Hebrew Antiquity," which he completed in the Department of Near Eastern Languages and Civilizations, for a doctoral committee composed of Peter Machinist (co-director), Ann Blair (co-director), and Jon Levenson (reader). The dissertation, and thus the book originated in a course Legaspi took on the history of biblical interpretation, taught by Machinist.[27] Machinist's influence, and that of Blair, a scholar of culture and intellectual history and the history of scholarship of early modern Europe, is detectable throughout, as is the influence of the other historians of biblical scholarship whom Legaspi acknowledges: Gary Anderson, James Kugel, Levenson, Jonathan Sheehan, Suzanne Marchand, Anthony Grafton, and Rudolf Smend.[28] Having read the original dissertation, which remains one of the most impressive I have read to date, I think this revised version is an improvement—better written, clearer, and with more force. These factors, combined with the importance and relevance of his volume's topic, warrant the following discussion in this chapter.

Legaspi's preface opens with an elegantly written page-and-a-half comparison of two "Bibles," what he terms the "scriptural Bible"—the Bible as encountered in sacred liturgy—and what he labels the "academic Bible"—the Bible as studied at the university.[29] As an example of the first, Legaspi uses his fine prose to paint a picture of an encounter with Scripture in the eastern liturgy of St. John Chrysostom.

> From behind the icon screen, the priest comes into view, carrying overhead, in solemn procession, an ornately bound, gold-plated volume: the Book of the Gospels. All stand. There is incense in the air. Acolytes, candles in hand, stand by to illuminate the reading of the Gospel. In that moment, the people are told not to look, to follow texts with their eyes, but rather to listen. The priest proclaims, "Wisdom! Let us attend!" and the people go silent.[30]

27. Legaspi, *Death of Scripture*, xii.
28. Ibid., xii–xiii.
29. Ibid., vii–xiv.
30. Ibid., vii.

Turning to the second example, the "academic Bible," Legaspi depicts a scene, familiar to Bible scholars—the biblical studies seminar classroom in a university setting.

> It too is filled with people. They sit, not stand. At the center is a long table. On it are many Bibles, various copies in assorted languages: Hebrew, Greek, Syriac, Latin. Some lie open, others are pushed aside into impromptu stacks. They share the table with other writings: teacher's notes, photocopies, reference works, dictionaries, grammars, commentaries. The atmosphere is sociable but cerebral, quiet but static. Heads are bowed, but over books. There are readers here too, but the oral performances are tracked closely by others whose eyes are attuned carefully to common texts.[31]

Legaspi's focus in this book is the story of the origin of the "academic Bible," which is why I selected him as our guide for this chapter; Legaspi's focus of study, Michaelis, is a founding figure in the history of the "academic Bible," as Legaspi describes it. Legaspi, however, locates the academic Bible's roots much earlier than Michaelis; Legaspi finds those roots back in the Reformation and its aftermath, "a moment when the scriptural Bible evoked by the liturgical scene above had already receded to the margins of modern Western cultural and public life."[32] Although the stage had been set for the "academic Bible" prior to the Enlightenment, it was not born until the eighteenth century. Legaspi explains, "The academic Bible was created by scholars who saw that the scriptural Bible, embedded as it was in confessional particularities, was inimical to the socio–political project from which Enlightenment universities drew their purpose and support."[33] Legaspi's basic thesis, which I find persuasive overall, is that, "The history of modern biblical criticism shows that the fundamental antitheses were not intellectual or theological, but rather social, moral, and political. Academic critics did not dispense with the authority of a Bible resonant with religion; they redeployed it."[34]

Michaelis, the eighteenth century biblical philologist, serves as Legaspi's case study. Michaelis proves to be important because he stands at the crossroads of the transformation we are discussing, but also because he is one of the most significant protagonists in the transformation itself.

31. Ibid.
32. Ibid., viii.
33. Ibid.
34. Ibid., xii.

In effect, Michaelis is one of the figures most responsible for the creation of modern biblical studies. The fact that Michaelis's theological views were rather traditional—he even adhered to the Mosaic authorship not only of the Pentateuch but also of the Book of Job—allows him to serve as a case in point that simple dichotomies such as secular versus religious are insufficient to grasp what was taking place in the eighteenth century.

Modern biblical criticism's early history dates from prior to the Reformation through the Enlightenment.[35] Legaspi argues that the Reformation killed Scripture, and that the Enlightenment attempted to revivify it.[36] Legaspi further elaborates, "the development of biblical studies as an academic discipline in Germany more than two hundred years after the Reformation was an outworking of what might be called the 'death of Scripture.'"[37] This death was in part a result of the textualization of Scripture, wherein Scripture ceased to be thought of primarily as a living Word with its primary home in the Liturgy, and became transformed into a book, eventually a dead historical book, a letter without the living Spirit which inspired it.[38]

Much of the criticism evidenced in the eighteenth century, already existed in the seventeenth century, in the writings of La Peyrère, Hobbes, Spinoza, and Simon.[39] In some sense, however, modern biblical studies at the university began in German-speaking lands during the Enlightenment built on this prior foundation. The methods and skill sets honed in eighteenth and nineteenth century German universities were already developed in France, England, and the Dutch Republic in the seventeenth century. German biblical criticism was somewhat of a late-comer to these

35. In summary fashion I tried to broaden this history from the late medieval period to the nineteenth century in Morrow, *Three Skeptics and the Bible*, 10–53. Elsewhere I showed how this history entered the Catholic world during the Modernist Crisis, ibid., "Modernist Crisis," 265–80; as well as in the fifth chapter of this present volume.

36. In Legaspi's words, "Scripture died a quiet death in Western Christendom some time in the sixteenth century. The death of scripture was attended by two ironies. First, those who brought the scriptural Bible to its death counted themselves among its defenders. Second, the power to revivify a moribund scriptural inheritance arose not from the churches but from the state. The first development was the Reformation, and the second was the rise, two hundred years later, of modern biblical scholarship." See Legaspi, *Death of Scripture*, 3.

37. Ibid., 4.

38 I attempt to describe this same process in Morrow, *Three Skeptics and the Bible*, 139–49.

39. On La Peyrère's role in this history, see ibid., 54–84. On Hobbes's place in this discussion, see ibid., 85–103. On Spinoza's importance, see ibid., 104–38. On all three, see also Morrow, "Acid of History." On Simon, see chapter 3 of this present volume.

critical methodologies, and yet, it was not until these methodologies were perfected at German Enlightenment universities that "an organized, institutional, and methodologically self-conscious critical program" was born.[40] Part of the impetus to this process was the splintering of Western Christendom at and following the Reformation. Scholastic and humanist debates within the Catholic world prior to the Reformation, and later Catholic and Protestant polemics, rendered the Bible opaque to would-be interpreters. Moreover, in the wake of the Reformation, and the skeptical erosion of biblical authority in works spanning La Peyrère on the one end, and Voltaire on the other, the Bible ceased to function as Scripture for many intellectuals in Western Europe.

Legaspi thus drives home to his readers:

> It was not simply deep curiosity about the language, form, and content of the Bible that spawned the ambitious research programs of eighteenth-century biblical scholars. In the decades surrounding the turn of the eighteenth century, the prestige of the Bible in the Western world was at an all-time low. Skeptics, rationalist critics, and proponents of the new science published widely and influentially on the state of its textual corruption, the unreliability of its historical narratives, the crudeness of its style, and, in some cases, the fanciful, even childish quality of its stories. . . . What developed in the mid-eighteenth century was not a new awareness of the "human" or "historical" character of the Bible. Rather, it was the realization that the Bible was no longer intelligible as scripture, that is, as a self-authorizing, unifying authority in European culture. . . . If the Bible was to find a place in a new political order committed to the unifying power of the state, it would have to do so as a common cultural inheritance.[41]

What German scholars in the newly formed Enlightenment universities did was redeploy the Bible for their cultural political projects, thus making it of contemporary relevance. Scholars like Michaelis essentially viewed the Bible as a dead historical text which informed modern audiences about a long dead historical civilization. Thus, its pages could be culled for clues that would aid the creation of a more robust German culture, and well-trained civil servants, loyal subjects of the state. As Legaspi explains, "They used historical research to write the Bible's death certificate while opening, simultaneously, a new avenue for recovering the biblical writings as ancient cultural products capable of reinforcing the values and aims of

40. Legaspi, *Death of Scripture*, 4.
41. Ibid., 4–5.

a new sociopolitical order. The Bible, once decomposed, could be used to fertilize modern culture."[42]

Following the work of Sheehan, Legaspi explains that, "The efforts of biblical scholars in this period must be understood as part of a larger attempt to shore up the authority of the Bible by rearticulating its cultural relevance and . . . by creatively demonstrating its value as a philological, moral, aesthetic, and historical resource."[43] In effect, the Reformation rendered the Bible unintelligible as Catholic Scripture—leaving in its carnage as many confessionally specific interpretations as denominations. Thus, the Enlightenment project attempted to create a new catholic (universal) Bible, by eschewing the various Scriptural Bibles born after the Reformation, and seeking instead a Bible as bedrock of Western civilization.

The Transformation of the University and of Classical Studies

The importance of the role of theology and the study of Scripture at universities like Göttingen, should not be underestimated in this context.[44] In fact, the University of Göttingen became the paradigmatic Enlightenment university. Legaspi explains that, "Over the course of the nineteenth century, academic theologians succeeded in assimilating theology to the realities of the modern state in order to ensure the continued survival of their discipline."[45]

Modern politics played an important role, not only in the creation of Enlightenment universities, but also in the transforming role of theology at the university, and in the creation of modern biblical studies. As Legaspi puts it:

> In the main, the guiding light of our eighteenth-century figures was not a beautiful vision of what criticism as a theological enterprise might look like. It was rather, for them, a matter of what biblical criticism, as a university subject, might *do*, what it might contribute to the education of men who would one day run the governments under which they themselves would have to live.[46]

---

42. Ibid., 5.
43. Ibid., 9.
44. See, e.g., ibid., 27–51.
45. Ibid., 29.
46. Ibid., 31.

The universities that originated or were reformed in the eighteenth century existed for the very purpose of serving the state. The *raison d'être* of German Enlightenment universities like Göttingen was to produce obedient civil servants. Following the work of Ian Hunter, whom he here quotes, Legaspi explains that the first of these new universities, Halle, was exemplary in "the way higher education in the period served the aims of 'a monarchical court bent on using [the university] to provide the state with a deconfessionalized ruling elite.'"[47]

One of the most crucial figures within this history, who helped pave the way for Michaelis, was theologian Johann Lorenz Mosheim (1693 to 1755). Mosheim helped set the theological program for Göttingen, and unlike many of his theological predecessors, he took the radical skepticism of the late seventeenth century seriously. He envisioned and embodied a theology that was interdisciplinary, and also advocated a broad interdisciplinarity at the university on theological grounds. Mosheim was completely opposed to theological controversies and debates, which he understood as internecine Christian polemics. As Spinoza had striven, at least ostensibly, for a scientific method of biblical interpretation that would end what he identified as religious conflict, so Mosheim sought to assess theological and religious matters with scientific precision. Michaelis would attempt to bring Mosheim's ideal into the realm of biblical scholarship. At the heart of this discussion is the turn to *Bildung* (culture).[48] Legaspi writes, "By turning to the category of culture, Göttingen scholars created a mode of *Wissenschaft* that also accorded with political gradualism, conservative reform, and a deep interest in what makes societies strong and distinct."[49] This was a scholarship bent on transforming all of German society by forming elite classically trained civil servants who would help the state direct the engines of modernity.

The parallels between biblical studies and classical studies have been selectively commented upon in the scholarly literature, but such discussions have been rather sparse.[50] More and more scholarly literature,

47. Ibid., 40. Legaspi here is relying upon Hunter, "Multiple Enlightenments," 579.

48. Legaspi describes the sense of *Bildung* in this context as "education and formation for the whole person." SeeLegaspi, *Death of Scripture*, 43.

49. Ibid., 51.

50. Some of the scholarly works that discuss a few of the connections between classical and biblical studies include Cassuto, *Documentary Hypothesis*, 11–14; Yamauchi, *Composition and Corroboration*; Grafton, "*Prolegomena*," 101–29 (ch. 9 of ibid., *Defenders of the Text*); Halpern, *First Historians*, 18; Van Seters, *Edited Bible*, xiv, 12, 19, 23–24, 27, 133–63, and 185–243; and Schwarzbach, "Eighteenth Century," 141–97. Legaspi does an excellent job of discussing the importance of classical studies as a paradigm for

however, has been demonstrating the importance of understanding the eighteenth century German turn to classical antiquity and pre-Christian Germanic culture to supplant any Catholic or Jewish heritage.[51] The time just before and during Michaelis's time at Göttingen was a key period in this history where German philhellenism influenced and completely transformed classical studies at the University of Göttingen.

Legaspi explains how, "German scholars, writers, and intellectuals looking beyond the Christian tradition turned to ancient Greece to recover an integrative vision of life. For several decades, Greek antiquity seemed to exercise a 'tyranny' over these figures and over German literature, philosophy, and religious thought."[52] This is how Göttinen became central to this story prior to Michaelis, precisely through the philological seminar which became the paradigmatic means of studying classical antiquity, and served as a model for later universities, like Berlin. As Legaspi observes, " . . . Göttingen at midcentury was not merely a way station on the road from seventeenth-century pedantry to nineteenth-century *Wissenschaft*. Rather, Göttingen must be seen as the site of an academic program with its own account of culture and belief, one shaped by the realities of the Enlightenment university."[53]

The thrust of the neo-humanist movement, which was born from philhellenism, was to refashion classical antiquity to serve as a practical model to reform contemporary cultural and political problems. The scientific study of classical antiquity, *Alterthumswissenschaft*, epitomized by Friedrich August Wolf (1759 to 1824) among others, required the mastery of the history and philology of Greek culture in order to dominate the material and redeploy it for contemporary German culture. The early German adherents of the philhellenism movement sought to delve into the world of ancient Greece. At the other end of this movement, neo-humanism sought to appropriate the gold of Athens, as it were, for the German present. The core of this neo-humanist project at Göttingen, was "aimed at

---

biblical studies in Legaspi, *Death of Scripture*, 53–78.

51. E.g., Marchand, *Down from Olympus*; Vick, "Greek Origins," 483–500; and Williamson, *Longing for Myth*. Legaspi explains that, "German philhellenism was not simply a movement: it was a 'faith.' To its proponents, it entailed the monumental task of replacing Christianity with a new form of life derived from an imaginative engagement with Greek antiquity." See Legaspi, *Death of Scripture*, 55.

52. Legaspi, *Death of Scripture*, 54.

53. Ibid., 55.

a renewal of culture based on a return to classical sources in their original languages."[54]

In this context, Johann Matthias Gesner (1691 to 1761), who pioneered his famous Philological Seminar at Göttingen, emerges as the paragon of classical scholarship. For Gesner, the study of ancient languages was merely a tool to enable students and scholars to make the content of texts accessible and thus useable for present cultural and political purposes. Gesner's approach would be very influential on Michaelis after the latter became his university colleague and the two became very good friends, and in fact Michaelis took over Gesner's Philological Seminar until a replacement was found. Eventually, Gesner was replaced by Christian Gottlob Heyne (1729 to 1812), who was responsible for transforming classical studies in a totalistic and holistic way. Heyne's approach to the investigation of classical antiquity was to employ every scholarly tool: art history, epigraphy, archaeology, mythology, religious and political history, etc. Michaelis would bring this methodology in the study of the Bible, creating the discipline of modern biblical studies.

Johann David Michaelis and the Birth of Modern Biblical Studies

Prior to Michaelis, the study of the Bible, even the study of Hebrew, had been primarily ancillary to theology.[55] Michaelis's genius made Hebrew philology and biblical studies their own separate and distinct disciplines severed from theological inquiry. Legaspi explains that, "Far from being an effort to promote abstractions like 'rationalism' or 'criticism,' Michaelis's recovery of Hebrew was an attempt to move beyond confessional interpretation and to render the Bible relevant as a new but old sort of cultural authority."[56] The rationale of Hebrew study for Michaelis was not primarily about correct biblical interpretation, but instead the enrichment of "European intellectual culture."[57]

One of Michaelis's fundamental moves was to emphasize the deadness of the Hebrew language. Prior to Michaelis, Christian Hebraism (the study of Hebrew and Jewish learning among Christians) had made recourse to Jewish learning on matters of Hebrew and related areas of knowledge.

54. Ibid., 61.

55. On Michaelis's Hebrew philology founded on the classical studies paradigm, see ibid., 79–104.

56. Ibid., 81.

57. Ibid., 84.

The assumption was that Jewish learning of Hebrew was superior to what Christians could learn on their own, because, in some way Hebrew was viewed as still a living language among European Jewry.[58] Even if Hebrew was not the "native" language of educated European Jews, since the study of the Hebrew Bible continued in Jewish communities, Christian scholars frequently sought out Jewish teachers.[59] With Michaelis's argument of the deadness of the Hebrew language, Christian scholars no longer needed the help of learned Jews. In fact, Michaelis brought a "periodization of Israelite and Jewish history" into the discussion, making a sharp separation within Israelite and Jewish history that would pave the way for later similar periodizations, which became fundamental to nineteenth century historical critical schemata.[60] Later Jewish history and learning was no longer important for understanding ancient Israelite texts.[61] What mattered according to Michaelis was not whether a scholar was Jewish or Christian, but instead insights into the workings of the Hebrew language were to be gained by comparing it with other Semitic analogues, especially Arabic which was a living Semitic language.[62]

According to Legaspi, "The systematic effort to interpret the Hebrew Bible ethnographically, in terms of present-day Arab language and culture, then, was one of the most distinctive features of Michaelis's program for

58. Even as late as about 1880 (thus prior to the advent of Modern Hebrew as a living language) Isaac Margolis taught his son, Max Margolis (famous Jewish Bible scholar and 1923 President of the Society of Biblical Literature), trigonometry and logarithms from a textbook, which he himself wrote, written in Hebrew. See Greenspoon, *Max Leopold Margolis*, 2.

59. Spinoza himself wrote a Hebrew grammar (which he never completed) for the aid of his non–Jewish friends, and which was later used by a number of Hebrew grammarians, including Wilhelm Gesenius, whose grammar remains in use today. See the studies, Klijnsmit, *Spinoza and Grammatical Tradition*; Klijnsmit, "Some Seventeenth–Century," 77–101; Klijnsmit, "Spinoza and the Grammarians," 155–200; and Rodrigues, "Algumas notas," 111–29. For Spinoza's grammar, *Compendium Grammatices Linguae Hebraeae*, see Spinoza, *Opera*, vol. 1.

60. Legaspi, *Death of Scripture*, 88.

61. Legaspi observes that, "In emphasizing the importance of ethnography and Near Eastern antiquities for the study of the Bible, Michaelis moved decisively away from what had been for centuries an obvious and important resource in biblical interpretation: Jews and Jewish literature. Christians had been learning Hebrew from Jewish teachers since the Middle Ages . . . . This situation lasted well into the eighteenth century, as even Michaelis's native Halle suggests . . . . It is striking, then, that Michaelis, who became the most eminent Orientalist and biblical commentator of his generation, flatly denied the relevance of Jewish learning to a *historical* or *philological* understanding of the Old Testament." See ibid., 96.

62. Ibid., 84–95.

Hebrew study and biblical interpretation."[63] Michaelis thus initiated an unprecedented state-sponsored expedition to Arabia.[64] This entire program had the effect of further separating his contemporary Jews from Christian Europeans.[65] For Michaelis, the Bible was to be viewed as any other ancient historical document, and thus could be accessible to the philologist apart from any theological standpoint. In this way, by imposing methodologies culled from classical studies, the Bible could be a source of enrichment, much like classical antiquity, for European culture.

Michaelis became a key means of importing English biblical criticism into the world of German scholarship.[66] This is particularly the case with the English critic Robert Lowth (1710 to 1787), for whom the biblical prophets became Hebrew poets. After showing how Rudolf Smend argues that Michaelis's editing of Lowth in German filtered Lowth through Michaelis's thought—so that, in a sense the German world got more Michaelis than Lowth—Legaspi demurs. Legaspi argues instead that, "Michaelis had clear insight into the true value of Lowth's work and that, as far as he knew, he was fully sympathetic to it," and he does this through showing how thoroughly English thought and culture influenced Michaelis.[67] Michaelis's time in England and the influence of English thought on him finds a later parallel with the later Scottish biblical critic William Robertson Smith (1846 to 1894), whose travels to Germany were so influential. As Michaelis brought much English biblical criticism to German scholarship, so Smith would later bring German biblical criticism to the English speaking world.[68]

63. Ibid., 95.

64. For more on the Danish Arabia Felix Expedition, see Sörlin, "National and International Aspects," 58–64; Vermeulen, "Anthropology in Colonial Contexts," 23–26; Hess, "Johann David Michaelis," 56–101; Sörlin, "Ordering the World," 65–67; Detalle, "Die dänische Expedition," 1–14; Carhart, *Science of Culture*, 27–68; Vermeulen, "Early History," 161–98; and Detalle and Detalle, "L'Islam," 487–543.

65. Legaspi, *Death of Scripture*, 97–101. For how this played out, again especially in German philological studies, in the nineteenth century as the field of comparative religion was born, see Masuzawa, *Invention of World Religions*.

66. Legaspi, *Death of Scripture*, 105–28.

67. Ibid., 117.

68. See, e.g., Rogerson, *Old Testament Criticism*; ibid., *Bible and Criticism*; Cheyne, "Bible and Confession," 24–40; Withrington, "School in the Free Church," 41–49; Morrison, "William Robertson Smith," 50–59; Hunter, "Indemnity," 60–66; Tomes, "Samuel Davidson," 67–77; Shiel, "William Robertson Smith," 78–85; Riesen, "Scholarship and Piety," 86–94; Kinnear, "William Robertson Smith," 95–100; Walls, "William Robertson Smith," 101–17; Bediako, "To Capture," 118–30; Rogerson, "W.R. Smith's *The Old Testament*," 132–47; Carroll, "Biblical Prophets," 148–57; Hadley, "William

The Mosaic Question and the Biblical Question

For Michaelis, Moses, as the national leader of Old Testament Israel during the exodus and wilderness period, would become the means of accessing and appropriating the cultural gold of Israel for Michaelis's Germanic present.[69] In this context, Michaelis's mammoth six-volume work, *Mosaisches Recht*, Michaelis' magnum opus published over a span of five years (1770 to 1775) is his most important work relating to this topic.

Moses exercised an important role in early modern political thought.[70] Legaspi explains that, "The Pentateuch became a resource for the study of leadership, political change, and statecraft. Biblical narrative was often stripped of its specific theological content and generalized to apply to contemporary political situations."[71] Moses played an especially pivotal role in the thought of Machiavelli and Spinoza. For Machiavelli, Moses was especially important as an exemplar for how to achieve a successful state.[72] For Spinoza, "Moses then became an absolute ruler."[73] Spinoza detected a "separation of powers" in the Mosaic legislation which matched his own views.

Robertson Smith," 164–79; Whitelam, "William Robertson Smith," 180–89; Day, "William Robertson Smith's Hitherto Unpublished," 190–202; Reif, "William Robertson Smith," 210–23; Smend, "William Robertson Smith," 226–42; Sæbø, "Some Problems," 243–51; Bailey, "William Robertson Smith," 252–63; Parman, "William Robertson Smith," 264–71; Douglas, "Demonology," 274–92; Rivière, "William Robertson Smith," 293–302; Boskovic, "William Robertson Smith," 303–10; Davies, "William Robertson Smith," 311–19; Lutzky, "Deity and Social Bond," 320–30; Philsooph, "Reconsideration of Frazer's Relationship," 331–42; Segal, "Smith versus Frazer," 343–51; Thrower, "Two Unlikely Travelling Companions," 383–89; Johnstone, "Legacy of William Robertson Smith," 390–97; Bediako, *Primal Religion*, especially 106–35; and Maier, *William Robertson Smith*, especially 86–122.

69. Legaspi, *Death of Scripture*, 129–53.

70. The role of Moses, and of Hebraic learning in general, in early modern European political thought, has thankfully become the focus of a whole host of recent scholarship. E.g., Schmidt–Biggemann, "Political Theology," 3–28; Lynch, "Machiavelli," 29–54; Neuman, "Political Hebraism," 57–70; Mittleman, "Some Thoughts," 72–89; Perreau–Saussine, "Why Draw," 90–104; Eyffinger, "How Wondrously," 107–47; Bodian, "Biblical 'Jewish Republic,'" 148–66; Lorberbaum, "Spinoza's Theological–Political Problem," 167–88; Rosenblatt, "Rabbinic Ideas," 191–206; Remer, "After Machiavelli," 207–30; Oz-Salzberger, "Political Thought," 231–56; Schochet, "Judeo–Christian Tradition," 259–82; and Nelson, *Hebrew Republic*.

71. Legaspi, *Death of Scripture*, 131.

72. See especially Marx, "Moses and Machiavellism," 551–71; Geerken, "Machiavelli's Moses," 579–95; Lynch, "Machiavelli," 29–55; and Remer, "After Machiavelli," 207–15 and 223–24.

73. Legaspi, *Death of Scripture*, 133.

Legaspi criticizes Spinoza's exegesis in places, most notably Spinoza's reading of Exodus 32, which Legaspi understands as "a willful misreading of the Golden Calf incident."[74] I would agree with Legaspi against Spinoza that what the text describes is not a case of "the vengefulness of the biblical god." But I do think Spinoza's exegesis of the replacement of the firstborn sons as priests with the Levites is correct. Legaspi writes:

> On the basis of a willful misreading of the Golden Calf incident (Exod 32), Spinoza attributes the decline of Israel to the vengeful, capricious character of the biblical god. Prior to the incident, he explains, Moses had entrusted religious leadership to firstborn sons throughout the tribes (Num 8:17). But after witnessing the idolatrous behavior of the Israelites, the biblical god lashed out against the people with the aid of sword–bearing Levites. He then stripped the firstborn of their ministry and made the Levites the priests of Israel, requiring that the people support them with gifts and offerings associated with the 'redemption' of the firstborn . . . . Though it was Moses and not God in Ex 32 who rallied the Levites and executed idolaters without explicit instructions to do so, Spinoza attributes the rise of the Levites and the concomitant decline of Israel to the vengefulness of the biblical god. In this way, he makes the biblical god the author of priestcraft and political disorder while saving the reputation of Moses as a philosopher attuned to the wisdom of the true God.[75]

Legaspi is right to criticize Spinoza here for his subtle attempt to justify his own political reading by denigrating the God of Israel in Exodus 32. In this passage, first-born sons serve as priests on account of their primogeniture, and are then replaced (after the fall of the golden calf) by the Levites because of the actions of these sword-wielding Levites. Spinoza's fundamental exegesis of the passage, however, does appear to explain the details of the text, at least in the final canonical form in which the text has come down to us. No one has made a better case for this than Scott Hahn in his rewritten doctoral dissertation, *Kinship By Covenant*.[76] Fathers and their firstborn sons apparently functioned as priests in the canonical Pentateuch prior to the golden calf incident.[77] Indeed, at the

74. Ibid.

75. Ibid., 133–34.

76. Hahn, *Kinship By Covenant*, especially chapter 6, "The Levitical Grant–Type Covenant," 136–75.

77. See ibid., 39–40 on the role of fathers as priests in the Old Testament and in the ancient Near East; and 136–42 on the priestly primogeniture of firstborn sons in

Passover in Egypt, God ransoms the firstborn sons of Israel. At the initial covenant God makes with Israel at Mt. Sinai in Exodus 24, we find "elders" functioning as priests (24:1 and 5), whom much of the Targumic literature interpreted as firstborn sons.[78] What the Levites did by splitting around 3,000 of their fellows in half, was, on this reading, enact the covenant curses (symbolized in the sacrificing of the animals and sprinkling of blood in Exod 24:5–6) triggered by the idolatry.[79] Thus, when we come to the Book of Numbers, we find the Levites ritually replacing the firstborn sons: first all of the people of Israel (other than Levites) are counted (Num 1); then the Levites are numbered separately from the people of Israel (Num 3:14–39); finally, all of Israel's firstborn sons (except from the Levites) are numbered (Num 3:40–43), and we read, "the Lord said to Moses, 'take the Levites instead of all the first–born among the people of Israel'" (Num 3:44–45, RSVCE), and money from the firstborn sons is handed over to the Levites (Num 3:46–51).[80] It would seem that Spinoza was correct at least as far as the replacement of the firstborn son priests with Levitical priests is concerned.

The history of pentateuchal criticism and the question of Moses, especially as it relates to Michaelis, is bound up with the work of Jean Astruc (1684 to 1766). Astruc's anonymous 1753 *Conjectures sur les mémoires originaux dont il paroit que Moyse s'est servi pour composer le Livre de la Genèse* was an attempt to defend the Mosaic authorship of the Pentateuch against earlier critics, namely La Peyrère, Hobbes, Spinoza, and Simon. What Astruc argued, however, was that Moses utilized ten minor sources, and two major ones, in composing Genesis through the beginning of Exodus. For Michaelis, Astruc had gone too far. Michaelis was suspicious of the neat-and-clean hypothetical sources Astruc deduced based on different names for God, etc. Michaelis conceded Moses's reliance on earlier sources, as well as minor editing by Joshua. Michaelis feared, however, that denials of Mosaic authorship would weaken the authority of the text, which was important to him for his cultural and political humanistic program. Moses was important to Michaelis because, as with Machiavelli and Spinoza before him, Michaelis saw in Moses the political ideals of his own time and place: namely, the subordination of church to state. The irony is

---

Genesis and Exodus.

78 See ibid., 44–48 on the covenant at Sinai in Exod 24.

79 See ibid., 51–56 on covenant oaths/curses and their ritual enactments.

80. See ibid., 146–47 on the golden calf episode causing the firstborn sons of Israel to lose their priestly status and triggering their replacement by the Levites.

that it was through Michaelis's critique of Astruc that Michaelis's own student, Johann Gottfried Eichhorn was made aware of Astruc's arguments, upon which Eichhorn would build thus setting the stage for the Documentary Hypothesis which came to full flower in the nineteenth century.

Michaelis bequeathed an important heritage to biblical studies, especially through his student Eichhorn, but he was not without his critics. Johann Georg Hamann's (1730 to 1788) perhaps offered the most trenchant contemporary critique of Michaelis.[81] Legaspi's concludes his volume with what he argued was the point of the Enlightenment creation of biblical studies:

> The scattered researches of earlier skeptics and freethinkers, though every bit as critical, did not coalesce into a compelling interpretive program until unified at the university. Guided by methods and assumptions that reinforced the statism and irenicism of the Enlightenment cameralists, the new discipline of biblical studies allowed practitioners to create a *post*-confessional Bible by reconstructing a *pre*-confessional Israel.[82]

In the next chapter we will bring this volume to a close by showing how modern historical biblical criticism entered the Catholic world during the Roman Catholic modernist crisis of the end of the nineteenth century and early part of the twentieth century. The focus in that final chapter will be on the separation of biblical studies from Catholic moral theology. My argument is it has much to do with the continuation of trends discussed in chapters 3 and 4, but specifically in light of the controversy over modernism in the Catholic world.

81. On Hamann and his critique of the new discipline of biblical studies, as well as Michaelis specifically, see Betz, *After Enlightenment*, especially 93, 99–104, 114–25, and 136–37; and ibid., "Glory(ing) in the Humility of the Word," 141–79.

82. Legaspi, *Death of Scripture*, 165.

5

A PARTING OF THE WAYS
Biblical Studies and Moral Theology

WITH NOTABLE EXCEPTIONS, MUCH of contemporary Catholic theology
proceeds in a fragmented way as if each branch developed in a hermeti-
cally sealed environment. Catholic theologians study and practice the
specific disciplines of systematic theology, historical theology, and moral
theology as if each were an isolated field. But no area of theology is so
cut off from other areas as that of biblical studies; the diverse theological branches mentioned above share the characteristic of being separated
from biblical studies.

Among biblical scholars in the academy, the Bible tends to be studied
almost as any other ancient document: Bible scholars pay careful attention
to its ancient history through studying Northwest Semitic philology, other
cognate languages like Akkadian, Egyptian, and Hittite; they attempt to
recover the Bible's long-gone formative matrices partially uncovered
through archaeology; they utilize comparative methodologies from ancillary fields; they run numerous textual variants through carefully con-
structed textual critical assumptions; and, even more than their colleagues
in ancient Near Eastern studies, they search for hypothetical original
sources that may have never actually existed outside of scholarly imagination. These are laudable areas of study, but they tend to be pre-theological.
This would not be a problem were it not for the lamentable fact that for
many scholars such methods have at times drawn attention away from
the integrity of the texts and even hindered theological understanding

of the Bible as Sacred Scripture, rather than aiding in such theological interpretations as necessary preliminary groundwork. In the last chapter we saw an important part of the history explaining the origin of this situation described above. Johann David Michaelis played an instrumental role in creating the modern discipline of biblical studies at the University of Göttingen. In what follows in this final chapter I describe the history of the separation of biblical studies from Catholic moral theology in the twentieth century and explore some of the negative consequences of this tragic separation.

Servais Pinckaers cautions:

> Scripture scholars . . . have fixed our attention a bit too much on human factors and on the cultural context which conditioned the sacred authors in their work of composition. We run the risk of forgetting that when we read Scripture, through this historic data we are placed before a Word that has mastery over time and that creates history, the history of a people that listens to it and of each believer personally, beginning with the most lowly. The Word leads them to an encounter with the living God. Certainly we should carefully take into account the historical and human envelope of Scripture, but this should not prevent us from seeing that in its substance it is formed by a Word that surpasses words, ideas, categories, and sentiments.[1]

Much of contemporary Catholic biblical scholarship has little to do with theology, and, in particular, it offers very little to the study of moral theology.[2] Likewise, much of contemporary Catholic theology, including moral theology, fails to engage biblical texts substantively, beyond an occasional highly selective appropriation of "assured" results of historical criticism, which often appear to be little more than proof-texting, utilizing only those conclusions of historical critical Bible scholars which fit neatly into a particular theological approach to ethics. This is particularly troublesome given the call of Vatican II in regard to moral theology: "Special care is to be taken for the improvement of moral theology. Its scientific presentation should be more based on the teaching of scripture, throwing light on the exalted vocation of the faithful in Christ and their obligation to bear fruit in charity for the life of the world."[3] Though this statement

---

1. Pinckaers, "Scripture and the Renewal," 62.

2. A noteworthy exception is Anderson, *Sin*.

3. *Optatum Totius*, no. 16. Citations from the documents of the Second Vatican Council are taken from Tanner, ed., *Decrees II*.

was no doubt addressing the neo-classicist manualism that reigned in moral theology at the time, despite the various changes in the five decades since Vatican II, theologians have continued to fail to make Scripture the "soul of sacred theology," as *Dei Verbum* taught.[4] David Fagerberg lays out the goal toward which we must strive: "Our task is to let the connection between liturgy, Scripture and theology be a path to a thickened understanding of each of them. That is what we have ceased doing because we no longer see these three in the light of the singular mystery of God."[5]

This present study traces the genealogy of how Catholic moral theology became divorced from biblical studies.[6] This story is inextricably linked with the Bible's separation from Catholic theology in general. The internal literary methods, often called historical-critical, for interpreting the Bible, despite how indispensable they have become, bear with them a political history that shapes the methods themselves so as to be in tension with traditional theological enterprises.[7] This article proceeds in three parts. The first part of this study assesses the recent history and current status of the Bible's separation from Catholic moral theology. The second portion runs through the history of the development of the literary historical-critical methods, underscoring the politics that often drove them. Within this second section, I will provide an overview of the Modernist controversy, showing that at heart this controversy was about how Catholic Bible scholars by and large uncritically appropriated these biblical methods. The final portion of this article explains how the response against Modernism conditioned Catholic Bible scholars virtually to ignore theology in their work. Subsequently, the near-hegemony of such biblical critical methods in the academy have made it very difficult for Catholic theologians, moral and otherwise, to engage deeply with Sacred Scripture.

The Divide Between of Scripture and Moral Theology

Prior to the Second Vatican Council, moral theology primarily took the form of manualism, and the study of moral theology was practiced by

4. *Dei Verbum*, no. 24.

5. Fagerberg, "Theologia Prima," 55.

6. Because others have discussed the role of certain forms of scholasticism and the manualist tradition in their accounts, I do not include them in my discussion here. See, e.g., Keenan, *History of Catholic Moral Theology*, 9–34; Gallagher, *Time Past*; Pinckaers, *Sources of Christian Ethics*, 254–79; and Gallagher, "Manual System," 1–16.

7. No one has shown this as forcefully as Hahn and Wiker, *Politicizing the Bible*.

self-identified "moralists," that is, priests whose chief objective was to train seminarians for their future task of hearing confessions, preaching on moral topics, and interacting with parishioners who might seek moral advice. Lest this seem to imply a narrow and restricted focus, it should be noted that these moralists did write on a large variety of topics both in academic journals and in popular magazines. A survey of essays on moral topics in *Theological Studies* prior to Vatican II confirms that an academic article written by a moralist was not a mere parsing of different Church laws and designation of culpability either mortal or venial to a penitent. Rather, moralists played a significant role to a variety of audiences, including political, popular, and ecclesial. Their conclusions influenced public policies, the decisions of Catholic institutions, bishops's agendas, and the perceptions of those lay people who encountered them either in the confessional or through their writings.[8]

On the other hand, there was a great deal of attention given to ecclesiastical law and the decisions and statements of the magisterium. Confession manuals served as handbooks of authority for making judgments on various "cases" that were representative of the sins encountered by a priest in a confessional. Fr. John C. Ford noted in an exam for his Jesuit seminarians that he did not want to test "abstract knowledge," but rather he wanted to gauge "the student's ability to apply correctly and prudently to concrete human situations the law and the moral principles and concepts he has studied for two years."[9] This skill was an important one for the priests who would be assisting the faithful in identifying their sins, assigning appropriate penances, and granting absolution. Though the sources for these manuals were Thomistic to some extent, (e.g., in their understanding of object, intention, and circumstances), they did not contain the regular reference to Scripture as seen in St. Thomas's *Summa Theologiae*. In fact, most manuals made no reference to Scripture, save for the occasional proof–text, and most moral theology done by moralists in this time period also made no reference to Scripture in any kind of systematic fashion.

This lack of Biblical reference was recognized as a problem by moral theologians prior to the council. One of the first to attend to this issue in extensive written form was the German Redemptorist Bernard Häring, author of the renowned 1954 work entitled *The Law of Christ*. John Gallagher describes the publication of *The Law of* Christ as a watershed in

8. See, for example, John McGreevy's description of the influence of Jesuit moralists John Ford and Gerald Kelly in McGreevy, *Catholicism and American Freedom*, 216–49.

9. Cited in ibid., 218.

the history of moral theology, setting in motion a process that ultimately resulted in the gradual removal of neo–Thomist manuals from seminaries in Europe and the United States.[10] Despite some criticism, this work was by and large received enthusiastically in Europe and the United States.[11] In particular, many noted that, in contrast to prior works in moral theology, Häring incorporated biblical passages into his work. This was recognized by moral theologians as an important effort to address the paucity of Scripture in prior texts of moral theology. Prior to Häring, the few who made mention of the Bible did so simply in order to back up a particular position that was already considered a part of natural law and often pre-served in ecclesiastical law as well.

But while Häring was lauded for his intent of making moral theology more Scriptural, *The Law of Christ* was also criticized for the manner in which Häring incorporated Scripture. Although not as selective as those who proof–texted passages on particular topics, Häring was criticized by some for his method of citing the Bible. John Lynch, summarizing the critiques of another scholar, in 1958 wrote: "As biblical theology, he submits, it is not genuine; its alleged Christocentrism is achieved merely by su-perimposing scriptural texts upon a garden variety of moral truths, many of which have been the target of recent criticism because of their aura of naturalism."[12] More recently, Jeffrey Siker has comprehensively evalu-ated Häring's two major works (*The Law of Christ* and *Free and Faithful in Christ*) and summarizes four basic uses of Scripture in Häring's work: 1) Proof-texting (using texts to support a position already established); 2) A biblical concept approach (choosing a theme such as "the heart" or "cov-enant" to highlight from Scripture); 3) Scripture as providing examples (using Gospel stories that illustrate moral points); and 4) Scripture as il-luminating (an almost homiletical use of passages that seems to invite one to further reflection).[13]

This first attempt at bridging the divide between Bible and moral theology is certainly commendable, but unfortunately it did not inspire a thorough reunification of the two fields. Rather, those who followed Häring continued to be weak in their use of Scripture, largely due to their limited and one-sided training in this area. One problematic aspect of Häring's use of Scripture, for example, is its selective nature, seemingly

10. Gallagher, *Time Past*, 169.

11. Lynch, "Notes on Moral Theology," 165.

12. Ibid.

13. Siker, *Scripture in Ethics*, 63–67.

based on little more than Häring's own preferences. This selectivity, how-ever, is somewhat inevitable for theologians like Häring who were not trained in Scripture, but yet believed they must take the courageous first step to try to reunite moral theology with biblical studies. Selectivity has remained a problem for those who followed Häring, however, as more recent theologians have similarly struggled in knowing which passages to use, exclude, or emphasize.

One important change that occurred during Häring's time was the move of academic moral theology from the seminary to the university, where more laity were becoming specialists in the field of moral theolo-gy.[14] No longer was moral theology restricted to the ordained; rather those studying the field were not destined for the confessional on the priest-side of the screen, and this association between the sacrament of confession and the study of moral theology seemed outdated, or, at least, unnecessary for lay scholars. Seminary formation was no longer assumed of those who became experts in moral theology; this meant that the laity pursuing this field did not have the extra theological, biblical, and homiletical training found in seminaries.

Many up and coming lay moral theologians were trained at Protes-tant institutions in "Christian ethics," but even those enrolled in theology programs at Catholic universities received biblical training of a particular genre. They were instructed in the historical-critical methods, emphasiz-ing various sources and the historical evolution of biblical texts. Moreover, the conclusions of these methods were more often taught as objective "fact" as in the hard sciences than as debatable literary hypotheses with evidence supporting various positions.

The confirmation of this particular understanding of the Bible can be found in the published texts of many recent moral theologians who, though recognizing the importance of the Bible for their work, have few resources to assist them in the theological interpretation of Scripture. Many well-regarded moral theologians simply fail to mention Scripture. Others will devote a single chapter to it as a particular resource for a topic. Often the Bible appears on equal-footing to the other texts being cited— such as UN reports on population statistics; in other words, the Bible is just another source to analyze, criticize, and select from at will.

Prior to his election as pope, Benedict XVI addressed what he saw as the tragic separation of Scripture from Catholic moral theology. Pope Benedict noted problems with the pre-conciliar manualist tradition's

14. Gallagher, *Time Past*, 197 and 199.

paucity of engagement with Scripture, but maintained that the situation is even worse after the Second Vatican Council. In light of initial post-conciliar attempts to engage with Scripture in Catholic moral theology, Pope Benedict observed:

> The foregoing explains the vicissitudes of post-conciliar moral theology, which has led to a radical heterogeneity of ends: while it was hoped that a renewed moral theology would go beyond the natural law system in order to recover a deeper bibli-cal inspiration, it was precisely moral theology that ended by marginalizing Sacred Scripture even more completely than the pre-conciliar manualist tradition.[15]

Benedict conceded that, "Biblical texts may appear in important and rich areas within the treatment of moral theology," but laments how, "their function, with regard to the constitution of moral action, is marginalized as a matter of principle."[16] Indeed, elsewhere Benedict observes that, "The Bible has to a great extent vanished from the modern works in moral theology."[17]

Benedict does not stand alone in his observations lamenting the trag-ic dearth of serious theology engagement with Scripture in post-conciliar Catholic moral theology. His predecessor Pope St. John Paul II issued his important papal encyclical on moral theology, *Veritatis Splendor*, in part to address this gap between Scripture and Catholic moral theology.[18] Pinckaers and Matthew Levering have likewise highlighted the ways in which moral theology has been cut off from its scriptural wellspring. In his work, Levering attempts to reunite the "book of Scripture" with the "book of nature" in order to help steer moral theology in a more fruitful direction.[19] Pinckaers, whose work represents a very important correc-tive in this direction, states emphatically that, "In my opinion the chief task for today's moral theologians is to reopen the lines of communication between Christian ethics and the Word of God."[20] For his part, Pinckaers concedes that many Catholic moral theologians by and large would agree

---

15. Benedict XVI, *Joseph Ratzinger in Communio I*, 187.

16. Ibid., 189.

17. Benedict XVI, *On Conscience*, 65.

18. John Paul II, *Veritatis Splendor*, no. 5.

19. Levering, *Biblical Natural Law*, 1.

20. Pinckaers, *Sources of Christian Ethics*, xviii.

with him, but he does not see sufficient evidence of the necessary changes taking place.[21]

Like the moralists of the 1950s, there are likely few moral theologians today who feel completely satisfied with in the contemporary usage of the Bible in the field of moral theology. But there are even fewer who know the history behind the present divide and the reasons for their limited graduate school encounter with biblical studies as the field now stands. The investigation contained in the next section of this article addresses that history and explains how the rift between moral theology and scriptural studies has continued to the current time, despite initiatives to reunite them in a constructive fashion.

Politics of Modern Biblical Criticism[22]

David Dungan provides a very telling auto-biographical confession:

> I had always thought that the historical-critical study of the Bible had nothing to do with politics, that it was a pure and noble calling requiring years of apprenticeship followed by decades of dedicated service in the vineyards of archaeology, comparative philology, historical reconstruction, sophisticated literary analysis, fearless theological critique, and so on. I never knew that I was a foot soldier in a great crusade to eviscerate the Bible's core theology, smother its moral standards under an avalanche of hostile historical questions, and, at the end, shove it aside so that the new bourgeois could get on with the business at hand. I had read Albert Schweitzer's warning that the historical study of the Bible originally had nothing to do with a genuine interest in history but appeared "as an ally in the struggle against the tyranny of dogma." But I dismissed his warning, perhaps because neither he nor any other historian ever spelled out in explicit detail how modern historical criticism of the Bible was originally forged as a weapon in the furious battle between the Enlightenment and the Christian Thrones and Altars of Europe. No one told me precisely how the inventors of the new historical method first eviscerated the Bible, then secretly packed it with their own values so that, after the defenders of orthodoxy had dragged this

21. Ibid., xviii.

22. For a more thorough treatment of this history, see Morrow, *Three Skeptics and the Bible*, 10–53.

strange Trojan horse inside their city, the hidden soldiers could
rule the city under the guise of biblical criticism.[23]

In the Christian world, as we saw in chapter 1, modern biblical criticism
began at least as early as the theo-political works of Marsilius of Padua and
William of Ockham as the pre-Reformation attempts to eclipse allegori-
cal exegesis. They attempted to curtail traditional forms of patristic and
medieval exegesis in order to curb the use of such interpretations which
supported the temporal authority of the papacy. Such arguments served
the court politics of Ludwig of Bavaria, under whose protection both Marsilius and Ockham resided together.[24]

The Renaissance and Reformation continued these trends, honing
philological and textual analyses.[25] It was in the seventeenth century, however, with the works of Isaac La Peyrère, Thomas Hobbes, Baruch Spinoza,
and Richard Simon that the foundations of modern biblical criticism
began to solidify with the dissolution of traditional attributions of authorship and its attendant skepticism regarding traditional theological biblical
interpretation.[26] La Peyrère used comparative historical analysis and what
he identified as contradictions in the biblical texts to dissolve traditional
attributions of authorship, interpretation, and authority. La Peyrère's motives were apparently to support the political machinations of the Prince of
Condé, whom he served as diplomat and secretary.[27] Hobbes, meanwhile,
argued for an historical interpretation of Scripture that naturalized the
supernatural in order to justify the status quo in England where the state
sovereign ruled both church and state within her realm.[28] Spinoza, upset
with the Jewish community who had ostracized him, turned against the
Hebrew Bible and Judaism with a vengeance, setting up a methodology
for biblical exegesis patterned on the natural sciences. His work was in

23. Dungan, *History of the Synoptic Problem*, 148.

24. Hahn and Wiker, *Politicizing the Bible*, 17–59; and Milbank, *Theology and Social Theory*, 17–20.

25. Kugel, "Bible in the University," 143–65; and Goshen-Gottstein, "Christianity,"
69–88.

26. Goshen-Gottstein, "Foundations of Biblical Philology," 77–94; and Goshen-
Gottstein, "Textual Criticism," 376.

27. Morrow, *Three Skeptics and the Bible*, 54–84; and Popkin, "Millenarianism and
Nationalism," 74–84.

28. Hahn and Wiker, *Politicizing the Bible*, 285–338; Morrow, *Three Skeptics and
the Bible*, 85–103; Reventlow, *Authority of the Bible*, 194–222; and Pacchi, "Hobbes and
Biblical Philology," 231–39.

support of the ruling class of the Dutch Republic.[29] Finally, as we saw in chapter 3, Simon continued the trajectory set by these contemporaries, as an apologetic in favor of Catholic tradition against Protestants in France; Simon's idea was that a Bible so full of such ridiculous errors required infallible Catholic tradition in order to make any theological sense. The works of these thinkers spread far and wide in the English speaking world.[30]

The eighteenth century saw English biblical scholarship based upon the methods of La Peyrère, Hobbes, Spinoza, and Simon enter the German-speaking world.[31] As we saw in the last chapter, German university systems were being erected to create model civil servants. Allegedly pure *Wissenschaft*, was thus an attempt to form a new generation of gentlemen scholars who would loyally serve the state, over and against the church if need be.[32] The work of Michaelis was paradigmatic here. Michaelis helped complete the transformation of the theological study of the Sacred Page into the completely cultural and historical discipline of biblical studies.[33]

By the nineteenth century, when most studies of the origin of historical biblical criticism begin their histories, German scholarship, which had been a late comer to modern biblical criticism, became the paragon of the academic study of Scripture.[34] Founded especially upon the classical scholarship of the previous century, nineteenth century German biblical criticism often went hand-in-hand with Prussian nationalism and with attempts to sever ties with a Catholic and a Jewish past, and instead search ancient Greece, Rome, and pre-Christian Germanic folklore for a firm foundation upon which to build a united national identity.[35] Such scholarship tended to assume that the presence of matters pertaining to priesthood, temple, sacrifice, and virtually anything else of the cultic or liturgical were later corruptions. Reformation polemics against Catholi-

29. Hahn and Wiker, *Politicizing the Bible*, 339–93; and Morrow, *Three Skeptics and the Bible*, 104–38.

30. Hahn and Wiker, *Politicizing the Bible*, 395–423; Champion, "Père Richard Simon," 39–61; and Woodbridge, "German Responses," 65–87.

31. Morrow, "Secularization, Objectivity, and Enlightenment Scholarship," 14–32; Gibert, *L'invention critique*, 309–16; Legaspi, *Death of Scripture*, 115–21; and Sheehan, *Enlightenment Bible*, 27–30.

32. Legaspi, *Death of Scripture*, 27–51; Hauerwas, *State of the University*, 6 and 12–32; and D'Costa, *Theology in the Public Square*, 8–20.

33. Legaspi, *Death of Scripture*, ix–xii, 79–153, and 155–65; Smend, *From Astruc*, 30–42; and Sheehan, *Enlightenment Bible*, 95, 135, 185–93, and 199–220.

34. Reventlow, *Epochen der Bibelauslegung 4*, 9 and 189.

35. Legaspi, *Death of Scripture*, 53–77; Marchand, *German Orientalism*; Williamson, *Longing for Myth*; and Marchand, *Down from Olympus*.

cism resurfaced in German biblical scholarship with abandon, and now Judaism became a target as well.[36] These trends continued explicitly into the twentieth century with calls to remove the Old Testament from the Christian Bible, and in at least one instance, replace the Old Testament with German folklore.[37] Predictably, such scholarship envisioned Jesus and the early disciples as Greco-Roman, and thus Indo-European, or Aryan as they were beginning to be called, and not Semitic.[38]

Catholic moral theology in the form of manualism underwent a parallel evolution during this time; it was within the context of the counter–Reformation that manuals of moral theology were developed to serve as instruments in the theological and ministerial education of Catholic priests.[39] Though these manuals evinced a lack of Scripture within their texts, it should not be assumed that this dearth ought to be attributed to scriptural controversies at the time. Rather, the manuals were a specific theological genre and are best understood in reference to their purpose of preparing priests as ministers of the sacrament of penance and administration of other sacraments; canon law was hence an important referent for these manuals.[40] The lack of biblical reference within the growing manualist tradition was not the result of any kind of anti-Scripture agenda, but rather, moral theology in the form of the pastoral training of priests did not seem to require the study of Scripture. The battle over the Bible was being fought in a different arena than that being used for seminary formation.

Manualism was a part of Catholic reformation in response to the criticisms of the Protestant Reformation; the Church recognized a weakness in the training of priests and found in the genre of manuals employed at the seminaries a manner of educating priests for their sacramental ministry, particularly in regard to judging moral issues in the confessional. The development of manuals was tied to transnational religious orders obedient to the pope and accountable to ecclesiastical laws; most especially the Jesuits developed the field of casuistry, but also important are the Redemptorists in the person of St. Alphonsus Liguori and the Dominicans

36. Jindo, "Revisiting Kaufmann," 41–77; Weinfeld, *Normative and Sectarian Judaism*, 286–90; Pasto, "W. M. L. de Wette," 33–52; and Pasto, "When the End," 157–202.

37. Arnold and Weisberg, "Centennial Review," 441–57.

38. Masuzawa, *Invention of World Religions*, xii–xiii, 24–6 and 145–206.

39. Gallagher, *Time Past*, 29. See also James Keenan's discussion of the *Summa Confessorum* as predecessors to the casuistry of the manuals in Keenan, *History of Catholic Moral Theology*, 2–3.

40. Gallagher, *Time Past*, 31–32.

had also contributed to the growth of moral manuals, and it was this Tridentine attempt to correct the Church failings that brought about pastoral and theological concerns at the time of the Reformation.

The advent of historical critical methods for Biblical interpretation, however, are best seen as a development from the Protestant Reformation, even though trends prior to the Reformation helped form and give shape to modern biblical criticism. While there were legitimate concerns about Catholic abuses of power causing scandal and neglect toward the faithful, the debates over the interpretation of Scripture often served political ends. Much of the political battle for power, in particular challenging the temporal authority of the pope, depended upon an interpretation of Scripture that would undermine papal authority and hence justify other state governments that were in no way accountable to ecclesial authority. As noted above, a number of the founding fathers of modern biblical criticism—Hobbes, Spinoza, Locke, et al.—found motivation in supporting particular local governments and certain leaders contra the transnational governance of the Catholic Church and the reign of the pope.

The Catholic Modernist Crisis[41]

The burgeoning discipline of historical-critical exegesis entered the world of Catholic biblical scholarship in a particular way. Although Catholics, like Marsilius of Padua, Ockham, and Richard Simon, played important roles along the way in developing modern historical biblical criticism, it remained primarily a Protestant exegetical tool founded on the theological basis of *sola Scriptura*. During and after the Enlightenment, such critical methodologies reached their modern form in German universities. The German biblical scholarship that produced a "higher anti-Semitism," as Solomon Schechter once called it, was an unfortunate byproduct of a much deeper political program whose main opponent was actually the Catholic Church, and particularly the papacy.[42] The long march to the birth of centralized modern European states in the seventeenth century coincided with the advent of modern biblical criticism.[43] Thus, it should come as no surprise that some of the same figures involved in justifying modern centralized states, and thus modern politics—Hobbes, Spinoza,

41. For a more thorough treatment of this history, see Morrow, "Modernist Crisis," 265–80.

42. Schechter, *Seminary Addresses*, 35–39.

43. See Morrow, *Three Skeptics and the Bible*, 139–49.

and John Locke—were also important figures in forging modern biblical criticism.[44]

The papacy looms large in the background of this debate because the papacy was viewed by state rulers, both Catholic and eventually Protestant, as a transnational authority which threatened rulers' claims to autonomy and sovereignty. At its foundation, modern politics set up the state as the new society which would organize time, labor, money, and discipline in opposition to the Church.[45] Likewise, at its core, modern biblical criticism was an attempt to wrest the Bible free from the authority of the Magisterium, and eventually also of Jewish and Protestant interpretive traditions, and place the interpretive authority solely in the hands of the university-trained scholar, who, in many cases was a servant of the state.[46] Thus, in a very real way such modern biblical criticism became nothing other than "state supported biblical scholarship."[47]

This is precisely how such historical criticism entered the Catholic world at large. Although Catholics had been involved in the rise of modern biblical criticism from the time of Marsilius and Ockham, much of the biblical studies of this nature remained primarily in the form of intra-church debates and proposed by a few individuals. However, at the end of the nineteenth century, these methodologies became widespread in the Catholic world. The work of Alfred Loisy became one of the most important examples of such scholarship. Like many of his contemporaries, Loisy attempted to examine the Bible apart from theology. He assumed that

44. Levenson, *Hebrew Bible*, 117.

45. Gross, *War Against Catholicism*; Duffy, *Saints & Sinners*, 193–94 and 203–4; and Portier, "Church Unity," 25–54. There are several important recent accounts underscoring the theological origins of such modern projects, e.g. Nelson, *Hebrew Republic*; and Gillespie, *Theological Origins of Modernity*. Despite their incredibly significant contributions, what these accounts miss is the very secularizing trends (e.g. theology's privatization and the subordination of church to state) inherent in such theological systems like Erastianism and even the various forms Protestantism represented by the magisterial reformers like Luther and Calvin.

46. The cases of Adolph von Harnack, Friedrich Delitzsch, and Gerhard Kittel are interesting to compare. Von Harnack argued for the removal of the Old Testament from the Christian Bible, and he served the Kaiser in drafting the letter defending Germany's entrance into World War I. Delitzsch followed von Harnack in his desire to remove the Old Testament, but went further in maintaining it should be replaced with German folklore, and he lectured at the Kaiser's palace and was involved in German colonial ambitions. Kittel was a member of the Nazi party and worked for the Nazi propaganda machine. See Meeks, "Nazi New Testament Professor," 513–44; Arnold and Weisberg, "Delitzsch in Context," 37–45; and O'Neill, "Adolf von Harnack," 1–18.

47. Farmer, "State *Interesse*," 24.

historical methodology was neutral and objective, and historical biblical criticism was free from commitment.[48]

Meanwhile, manualism's development had continued in isolation from Scripture, but, again, not because of any presumption against Scripture, per se, but only because the purpose of the genre did not lend itself to the consideration of scriptural debates. While moral theology was an ever–expanding field, it expanded in order to address new issues of morality or those most common in particular geographic regions. While this genre was increasingly criticized for various failures, such as neglecting the supernatural end, being overly focused on determining levels of sin and punishment for them, being too legalistic and encouraging a minimalist morality, it was not until the mid–twentieth century that moralists really became concerned about the lack of scriptural presence in the manuals.

Openness to Historical Criticism

The divorce of theology and ethics from the Bible within the Catholic world solidified during the period of the Modernist controversy. Pope St. Pius X's 1907 *Pascendi Dominici Gregis* condemned rationalistic examinations of the Bible that sought to emphasize historicity at the expense of the faith. In the reaction to Modernism which followed, many of the measures taken to stamp out Modernism were harsh.[49] In particular, the clandestine operations of the Sodalitium Pianum were a frightening threat to scholars. This organization was ultimately suppressed by St. Pius X's successor Pope Benedict XV, who had himself been suspected of being a Modernist, as apparently was Angelo Roncalli, later Pope St. John XXIII.[50] The Sodali-

48. On Loisy's biblical criticism, see Morrow, "Alfred Loisy's Developmental Approach," 324–44; Morrow, "Alfred Loisy and les Mythes Babyloniens," 87–103; and Talar, "Innovation and Biblical Interpretation," 191–211; and Talar, *(Re)reading, Reception, and Rhetoric,* 83–126.

49. The nineteenth century political background, however, helps provide some insight into the response against Modernism. In response to numerous threats, Pope Gregory XVI asked Austria to invade and occupy the Papal States. After Pius IX replaced Gregory as pope, the Piedmontese revolutionaries asked Pope Pius to join their forces against the Austrians, which the Pope refused. In retaliation, they assassinated the prime minister of the Papal States while he was holding parliament. The Piedmontese eventually wrested the region from the Catholic Church, bringing an end to the Papal States and cutting short the First Vatican Council. By the time of Pius X, Modernism was viewed within this historical–political context, not least because Modernist literature was being used by revolutionary political parties. See Lease, "Vatican Foreign Policy," 31–55.

50. Portier, *Divided Friends,* 51–64; Jodock, "Introduction II," 27; O'Connell, *Critics*

tium Pianum's anonymous denouncements of Catholic professors created a climate of hostility and terror throughout Europe and the United States. It was not a good time for moral theologians to take an interest in the Bible, as any and all academic study seemed to involve one in scrutiny of the highest degree.

When this period of anti-Modernist hostility ended with the Second Vatican Council (1962 to 1965), Catholic Bible scholars still had to fight to be recognized by the non-Catholic guild as true scholars. Much of non-Catholic biblical scholarship in the past had been done with the intent of questioning Catholicism's power; inherent in this mode of biblical scholarship was the assumption that being Catholic was a dangerously blinding bias that prevented an objective and scientific reading of Scripture. Catholic scholars of the Bible, free of the previous generation's fear of censure, sought to counter this stereotype by embracing the "scientific" methods now regarded as yielding factual results, but they also were careful to avoid relating their study to theological conclusions, which had been the concern of the Modernist controversy.

The controversy over Modernism had seemed to reinforce the scholarly limits placed on academics who studied the Bible. With limited options and the hope for acceptance in biblical studies at large, the new generation of Catholics desiring to study the Bible fled to philology and historical reconstruction at non-Catholic institutes like Johns Hopkins University. Not only would such a location remove them from the inhospitable climate for theological engagement with Scripture, it would also provide an avenue for Catholics to prove themselves capable of the most sophisticated linguistic and historical analysis.[51] Many did succeed in this study of the Bible, meaning that Catholic Scripture scholars of this generation were in no way trained for theological interpretation, unless, like Fr. Raymond Brown, they had already received specific theological training beforehand in their course of studies; this became progressively less frequent as more and more Catholic Bible scholars were laymen and laywomen As they became teachers, they passed on the non-theological knowledge and methods that they had gained. Moreover, deprived of a theological endeavor, such biblical study tended to see the historical-critical methods—which had once seemed off-limits—as the standards of biblical study, with hypothetical literary theories being prized as of chief importance, rather than as one method among others of equal standing.

---

on Trial, 321, 341, 348n68, 361–65; and Rivière, Le Modernisme, 469.

51. See, e.g., the comments in Johnson, "What's Catholic," 3–34.

By this point, at the end of the Second Vatican Council, only specialists were encouraged to handle Scripture at an advanced level. Within two
decades, the majority of theologians, moral and otherwise, were no longer
primarily priests and religious, but laypeople who had studied Scripture
and theology in near complete isolation and with a bias in favor of the
historical-critical methods developed in contexts hostile to the Church. So
also theology rarely entered the Bible classroom, other than in discussions
of the alleged historical positions of hypothetical authors or communities
assumed to be responsible for fragments and segments of various strata in
biblical narratives.

The moral theologians, increasingly lay, who were trained in the
wake of Vatican II were left to encounter Scripture study in this historical-
critical form. Whether at Catholic or Protestant institutions, such methods
of biblical study were hegemonic, with very little inquiry into the motivation for their origins. In an unfortunate coincidence of history, Catholic
moral theologians were being asked to enrich their field with Scripture
precisely at a time when Catholic biblical studies were most openly antithetical to theological concerns. Still rebounding from the Modernist
controversy, and with a paucity of Catholic biblical scholarship that was
theological during that time period, Catholic Scripture scholars were not
in the best position to assist moral theologians in learning how to relate
the moral truths of manuals to the Bible. Given a choice between dig-
ging through what was dismissed as the "pre-critical" biblical exegesis of
the Fathers and the modern historical criticism presented to them as the
product of science in the classroom, moral theologians found themselves
more often employing the latter methods of interpretation which were
the only deemed respectable. Since these methods were developed as pre-
theological, often anti-theological, and since they remained isolated from
theology, they offered very little to those looking for insight to address
moral problems.

The separation of the Bible from Catholic moral theology is a regret-
table development. When we look back in history to theologians like St.
Thomas Aquinas, we find masters of the Sacred Page. With the ever–more
specialized theological and historical disciplines, such inter-field flu-
ency is impossible. Catholic moral theologians, nevertheless, must engage
with Scripture beyond merely superficial readings. The historical-critical
method was developed to take Scripture out of the hands of Catholic, and
later even non-Catholic, theologians and place the Bible in the hands of
philological, textual, and historical specialists serving the needs of ever

more anti-clerical states. Such pretensions of neutrality must be unmasked for what they are. Historical criticism's façade of objectivity is no more attainable than, in Peter Novick's words, "nailing jelly to the wall."[52] As Jon Levenson explains, "the secularity of historical criticism represents not the suppression of commitment, but its relocation."[53] With the Modernist controversy and its aftermath prior to the Second Vatican Council, we find the near hegemonic status of modern biblical criticism curtailing attempts at reading Scripture theologically. We need to find a means of surmounting this impasse.

52. I borrowed this metaphor from Novick, *That Noble Dream*, 7.
53. Levenson, *Hebrew Bible*, 125.

CONCLUSION

STUDYING THE HISTORY OF modern biblical scholarship helps us better understand the roots of modern methods of exegesis. Many lessons can be learned from such an investigation. The often hidden role politics plays behind the scenes has been increasingly recognized as biblical scholars delve deeper into the history of their discipline. One thing that should be clear is that theologians should not fear to read the Bible theologically, as if only pre-theological historical-critical methodologies were appropriate for reading Scripture rightly.

In this volume, we have taken a broad look at various important segments from within the history of modern biblical criticism. In chapter 1, taking our cues from the work of Scott Hahn and Benjamin Wiker, we surveyed some of the underappreciated pre-history of modern biblical criticism from 1300 to 1700.[1] In that survey we saw some of the specific philosophies and politics, which too often go unrecognized, that helped shape and give rise to the methods that developed into modern biblical criticism in the work of key players in this history, many of whom are ignored in the scholarly literature: Marsilius of Padua (1275 to 1342); William of Ockham (1285 to 1347); John Wycliffe (1320 to 1384); Niccolò Machiavelli (1469 to 1527); Martin Luther (1483 to 1546); King Henry VIII (1491 to 1547); René Descartes (1596 to 1650); Thomas Hobbes (1588 to 1679); Baruch Spinoza (1632 to 1677); Richard Simon (1638 to 1712); John Locke (1632 to 1704); and John Toland (1670 to 1722).

In chapter 2, we took a closer look at Spinoza and the way in which his use of the Psalms in his *Tractatus theologico-politicus* fit within the overarching framework of his political program. In chapter 3 we looked at Richard Simon and St. Thomas More (1478 to 1535). Many look to Simon as a better and more faithful theological response to Spinoza's more

---

1. Hahn and Wiker, *Politicizing the Bible*.

destructive skeptical exegetical program. I argued, however, that Simon's work was merely a continuation of Spinoza's and thus more of a Trojan horse for Spinoza's method than a higher road to travel. I turned to St. Thomas More's earlier integration of faith and reason as a better path than Simon's.

In chapter 4 we followed Michael Legaspi's lead and looked at Johann David Michaelis's (1717 to 1791) role at the University of Göttingen in helping to form and solidify modern biblical studies at the Enlightenment university which secured such biblical studies a place in the future academy.[2] Finally, in chapter 5 we looked at the separation of the study of Sacred Scripture from Catholic moral theology in the twentieth century. I pointed to the modernist crisis as a key moment in the history of Catholic biblical scholarship when Catholic biblical scholars began to embrace the methods of historical criticism forged in the prior centuries.

For those seeking to integrate theology and biblical exegesis, history obviously cannot be ignored. Nor must the texts of Scripture remain in the historical past of long ago. Rather, the historical investigation should aid in a better understanding of Scripture, its background, culture, language, etc. For the theologian, and for any Christian, the study of the Sacred Page should above all lead to an encounter with God. Reading Scripture, moreover, must become one form of this great encounter.

2. Legaspi, *Death of Scripture*.

BIBLIOGRAPHY

Ackroyd, Peter. *The Life of Thomas More*. London: Chatto & Windus, 1998.

Adang, Camilla. "Schriftvervalsing als thema in de islamitische polemiek tegen het jodendom." *Ter Herkenning* 16.3 (1988) 190–202.

———. "Some Neglected Aspects of Medieval Polemics against Christianity." *Harvard Theological Review* 89.1 (1996) 61–84.

———. "*Taḥrīf* and Thirteen Scrolls of Torah." *Jerusalem Studies in Arabic and Islam* 18 (1992) 81–88.

Algermissen, Ernest. "Die Pentateuchzitate Ibn Hazms. Ein beitrag zur Geschichte der arabische Bibelübersetzungen." Thesis, Westfälische Wilhelms-Universität, Münster, 1933.

Anderson, Gary A. *Sin: A History*. New Haven: Yale University Press, 2009.

Armogathe, Jean-Robert, ed. *Le Grand Siècle et la Bible*. Paris: Beauchesne, 1989.

Arnaldez, Roger. "Spinoza et la pensée arabe." *Revue de Synthèse* 89–91 (1978) 151–74.

Arnold, Bill T., and David B. Weisberg. "A Centennial Review of Friedrich Delitzsch's 'Babel und Bibel' Lectures." *Journal of Biblical Literature* 121.3 (2002) 441–57.

———. "Delitzsch in Context." In vol. 2 of *God's Word for Our World*, edited by J. Harold Ellens, Deborah L. Ellens, Rolf P. Knierim, and Isaac Kalimi, 37–45. London: T. & T. Clark, 2004.

Asad, Talal. *Genealogies of Religion: Discipline and Reasons of Power in Christianity and Islam*. Baltimore: Johns Hopkins University Press, 1993.

Auvray, Paul. "Richard Simon et Spinoza." In *Religion, érudition et critique à la fin du XVII e siècle et au début du XVIIIe*, edited by Baudouin de Gaiffier, Bruno Neveu, René Voeltzel, and Jacques Solé, 201–14. Paris: Presses universitaires de France, 1968.

Bailey, Warner M. "William Robertson Smith and the Revival of American Biblical Studies." In *William Robertson Smith: Essays in Reassessment*, edited by William Johnstone, 252–63. Sheffield: Sheffield Academic, 1995.

Baird, William. *History of New Testament Research*. Vol. 1, *From Deism to Tübingen*. Minneapolis: Augsburg Fortress, 1992.

Barron, Caroline M. "The Making of a London Citizen." In *The Cambridge Companion to Thomas More*, edited by George M. Logan, 3–21. Cambridge: Cambridge University Press, 2011.

Barthélemy, Dominique, ed. *Critique textuelle de l'Ancien Testament 1: Josué, Juges, Ruth, Samuel, Rois, Chroniques, Esdras, Néhémie, Esther*. Fribourg: Editions Universitaires; Göttingen: Vandenhoeck & Ruprecht, 1982.

————, ed. *Critique textuelle de l'Ancien Testament 2: Isaïe, Jérémie, Lamentations.* Fribourg: Editions Universitaires; Göttingen: Vandenhoeck & Ruprecht, 1986.

————, ed. *Critique textuelle de l'Ancien Testament 3: Ezéchiel, Daniel et les 12 Prophètes.* Fribourg: Editions Universitaires; Göttingen: Vandenhoeck & Ruprecht, 1992.

————, ed. *Critique textuelle de l'Ancien Testament 4: Psaumes.* Fribourg: Editions Universitaires; Göttingen: Vandenhoeck & Ruprecht, 2005.

————, ed. *Critique textuelle de l'Ancien Testament 5: Job, Proverbes, Qohélet et Cantique des Cantiques.* Fribourg: Editions Universitaires; Göttingen: Vandenhoeck & Ruprecht, 2016.

————. *Studies in the Text of the Old Testament: An Introduction to the Hebrew Old Testament Text Project: English Translation of the Introductions to Volumes 1, 2, and 3 Critique textuelle de l'Ancien Testament.* Winona Lake: Eisenbrauns, 2012.

Barton, John. *The Old Testament: Canon, Literature and Theology.* Aldershot: Ashgate, 2007.

Bediako, Gillian M. *Primal Religion and the Bible: William Robertson Smith and His Heritage.* Sheffield: Sheffield Academic, 1997.

————. "'To Capture the Modern Universe of Thought': *Religion of the Semites* as an Attempt at a Christian Comparative Religion." In *William Robertson Smith: Essays in Reassessment,* edited by William Johnstone, 118–30. Sheffield: Sheffield Academic, 1995.

Belaval, Yvon, and Dominique Bourel, eds. *Le siècle des Lumières et la Bible.* Paris: Beauchesne, 1986.

Benedict XVI, Pope (Joseph Ratzinger). *Jesus of Nazareth.* Part I, *From the Baptism in the Jordan to the Transfiguration.* New York: Doubleday, 2007.

————. *Jesus of Nazareth.* Part II, *Holy Week: From the Entrance into Jerusalem to the Resurrection.* San Francisco: Ignatius, 2011.

————. *Joseph Ratzinger in Communio.* Vol. 1, *The Unity of the Church.* Grand Rapids: Eerdmans, 2010.

————. "Kirchliches Lehramt und Exegese. Reflexionen aus Anlass des 100–jährigen Bestehens der Päpstlichen Bibelkommission." *Internationale Kathlische Zeitschrift: Communio* 32 (2003) 522–29.

————. *On Conscience.* San Francisco: Ignatius, 2007.

————. *Schriftsauslegung im Widerstreit.* Freiburg im Breisgau: Herder, 1989.

————. "Verbum Domini." *Acta Apostolicae Sedis* 102 (2010) 681–787.

Berglar, Peter. *Thomas More: A Lonely Voice against the Power of the State.* Princeton: Scepter, 2009.

Berlin, Charles, and Aaron L. Katchen, eds. *Christian Hebraism: The Study of Jewish Culture by Christian Scholars in Medieval and Early Modern Times.* Cambridge: Harvard University Library, 1988.

Bernier, Jean. *La critique du Pentateuque de Hobbes à Calmet.* Paris: Champion, 2010.

————. "Richard Simon et l'hypothèse des écrivains publics: Un échec humiliant." *Revue d'histoire et de philosophie religieuses* 87 (2007) 157–76.

Betz, John R. *After Enlightenment: The Post-Secular Vision of J. G. Hamann.* Oxford: Wiley-Blackwell, 2009.

————. "Glory(ing) in the Humility of the Word: The Kenotic Form of Revelation in J. G. Hamann." *Letter & Spirit* 6 (2010) 141–79.

Blank, Reiner. *Analyse und Kritik der formgeschichtlichen Arbeiten von Martin Dibelius und Rudolf Bultmann.* Basel: F. Reinhardt, 1981.

Bodian, Miriam. "The Biblical 'Jewish Republic' and the Dutch New Israel in Seventeenth-Century Dutch Thought." In *Political Hebraism: Judaic Sources in Early Modern Political Thought*, edited by Gordon Schochet, Fania Oz-Salzberger, and Meirav Jones, 148–66. Jerusalem: Shalem, 2008.

Boskovic, Aleksandar. "William Robertson Smith and the Anthropological Study of Myth." In *William Robertson Smith: Essays in Reassessment*, edited by William Johnstone, 303–10. Sheffield: Sheffield Academic, 1995.

Burnett, Steven G. *From Christian Hebraism to Jewish Studies: Johannes Buxtorf (1564–1629) and Hebrew Learning in the Seventeenth Century.* Leiden: Brill, 1996.

Camporeale, Salvatore I. "Da Lorenzo Valla a Tommaso Moro: Lo statuto umanistico della teologia." *Memorie domenicane* 4 (1973) 9–102.

Carhart, Michael C. *The Science of Culture in Enlightenment Germany.* Cambridge: Harvard University Press, 2007.

Carroll, Robert P. "The Biblical Prophets as Apologists for the Christian Religion: Reading William Robertson Smith's *The Prophets of Israel* Today." In *William Robertson Smith: Essays in Reassessment*, edited by William Johnstone, 148–57. Sheffield: Sheffield Academic, 1995.

Cassuto, Umberto. *The Documentary Hypothesis and the Composition of the Pentateuch: Eight Lectures.* Jerusalem: Magness, 2006 (1941).

Cavanaugh, William T. "'A Fire Strong Enough to Consume the House': The Wars of Religion and the Rise of the State." *Modern Theology* 11 (1995) 397–420.

———. *The Myth of Religious Violence: Secular Ideology and the Roots of Modern Conflict.* Oxford: Oxford University Press, 2009.

Champion, Justin A. I. "Père Richard Simon and English Biblical Criticism, 1680–1700." In *Everything Connects: In Conference with Richard H. Popkin: Essays in His Honor*, edited by James E. Force and David S. Katz, 39–61. Leiden: Brill, 1999.

Cheyne, Alec C. "Bible and Confession in Scotland: The Background to the Robertson Smith Case." In *William Robertson Smith: Essays in Reassessment*, edited by William Johnstone, 24–40. Sheffield: Sheffield Academic, 1995.

Childs, Brevard S. "Wellhausen in English." *Semeia* 25 (1982) 83–88.

Coleman, Frank M. "Thomas Hobbes and the Hebraic Bible." *History of Political Thought* 25.4 (2004) 642–69.

Cooke, Paul D. *Hobbes and Christianity: Reassessing the Bible in Leviathan.* Lanham, MD: Rowman & Littlefield, 1996.

Coudert, Allison. *Hebraica Veritas?: Christian Hebraists and the Study of Judaism in Early Modern Europe.* Philadelphia: University of Pennsylvania Press, 2004.

Curtis, Cathy. "More's Public Life." In *The Cambridge Companion to Thomas More*, edited by George M. Logan, 69–92. Cambridge: Cambridge University Press, 2011.

Dahl, Nils A. "Wellhausen on the New Testament." *Semeia* 25 (1982) 89–110.

Davies, Douglas. "William Robertson Smith and Frank Byron Jevons: Faith and Evolution." In *William Robertson Smith: Essays in Reassessment*, edited by William Johnstone, 311–19. Sheffield: Sheffield Academic, 1995.

Day, John. "William Robertson Smith's Hitherto Unpublished Second and Third Series of Burnett Lectures on the Religion of the Semites." In *William Robertson Smith: Essays in Reassessment*, edited by William Johnstone, 190–202. Sheffield: Sheffield Academic, 1995.

D'Costa, Gavin. *Theology in the Public Square: Church, Academy and Nation.* Malden, MA: Blackwell, 2005.

Detalle, Michel-Pierre. "Die dänische Expedition nach Arabien, C. Niebuhr und Frankreich." *Historische Mitteilungen der Ranke-Gesellschaft* 16 (2003) 1–14.

Detalle, Michel-Pierre, and Renaud Detalle. "L'Islam vu par Carsten Niebuhr, voyageur en Orient (1761–1767)." *Revue de l'histoire des religions* 225.4 (2008) 487–543.

Diamond, James Arthur. "Maimonides, Spinoza, and Buber Read the Hebrew Bible: The Hermeneutical Keys of Divine 'Fire' and 'Spirit' (*Ruach*)." *Journal of Religion* 91 (2011) 320–43.

Douglas, Mary. "Demonology in William Robertson Smith's Theory of Religious Belief." In *William Robertson Smith: Essays in Reassessment*, edited by William Johnstone, 274–92. Sheffield: Sheffield Academic, 1995.

Duffy, Eamon. "'The Common Knowen Multytude of Crysten Men': *A Dialogue Concerning Heresies* and the Defence of Christendom." In *The Cambridge Companion to Thomas More*, edited by George M. Logan, 191–215. Cambridge: Cambridge University Press, 2011.

———. *Saints & Sinners: A History of the Popes.* 3rd ed. New Haven: Yale University Press, 2006.

———. *The Stripping of the Altars: Traditional Religion in England c. 1400–c. 1580.* New Haven: Yale University Press, 1992.

———. *The Voices of Morebath: Reformation & Rebellion in an English Village.* New Haven: Yale University Press, 2001.

Dungan, David Laird. *A History of the Synoptic Problem: The Canon, the Text, the Composition, and the Interpretation of the Gospels.* New York: Doubleday, 1999.

Eyffinger, Arthur. "'How Wondrously Moses Goes Along with the House of Orange!': Hugo Grotius' 'De Republica Emendanda' in the Context of the Dutch Revolt." In *Political Hebraism: Judaic Sources in Early Modern Political Thought*, edited by Gordon Schochet, Fania Oz-Salzberger, and Meirav Jones, 107–47. Jerusalem: Shalem, 2008.

Fagerberg, David W. "Theologia Prima: The Liturgical Mystery and the Mystery of God." *Letter & Spirit* 2 (2006) 55–67.

Farmer, William R. "State *Interesse* and Markan Primacy: 1870–1914." In *Biblical Studies and the Shifting of Paradigms, 1850–1914*, edited by Henning Graf Reventlow and William Farmer, 15–49. Sheffield: Sheffield Academic, 1995.

Fatio, Olivier, and Pierre Fraenkel, eds. *Histoire de l'exégèse au XVIe siècle.* Geneva: Librairie Droz, 1978.

Fleyfel, Antoine. "Richard Simon, critique de la sacralité biblique." *Revue d'histoire et de philosophie religieuses* 88 (2008) 469–92.

Force, James E., and Richard H. Popkin, eds. *The Books of Nature and Scripture: Recent Essays on Natural Philosophy, Theology, and Biblical Criticism in the Netherlands of Spinoza's Time and the British Isles of Newton's Time.* Dordrecht: Kluwer Academic, 1994.

Frampton, Travis L. *Spinoza and the Rise of Historical Criticism of the Bible.* London: T. & T. Clark, 2006.

Freedman, R. David. "The Father of Modern Biblical Scholarship." *Journal of the Ancient Near Eastern Society* 19 (1989) 31–38.

Frei, Hans W. *The Eclipse of the Biblical Narrative: A Study in Eighteenth and Nineteenth Century Hermeneutics.* New Haven: Yale University Press, 1974.

Gabbey, Alan. "Spinoza's Natural Science and Methodology." In *The Cambridge Companion to Spinoza*, edited by Don Garrett, 142–91. Cambridge: Cambridge University Press, 1996.

Gallagher, John A. *Time Past, Time Future: An Historical Study of Catholic Moral Theology*. Eugene, OR: Wipf & Stock, 1990.

Gallagher, Raphael. "The Manual System of Moral Theology Since the Death of Alphonsus." *Irish Theological Quarterly* 51 (1985) 1–16.

Garrido Zaragoza, J. "La desmitificación de la Escritura en Spinoza." *Taula* 9 (1988) 3–45.

Gasque, W. Ward. *A History of the Criticism of the Acts of the Apostles*. Tübingen: Mohr, 1975.

Geerken, John H. "Machiavelli's Moses and Renaissance Politics." *Journal of the History of Ideas* 60.4 (1999) 579–95.

Gibert, Pierre. Introduction à la présente édition, *Histoire critique du Vieux Testament, suivi de Lettre sur l'inspiration: Nouvelle edition*, by Richard Simon, edited by Pierre Gibert, 11–63. Montrouge: Bayard, 2008.

———. *L'invention critique de la Bible: XVe – XVIIIe siècle*. Paris: Gallimard, 2010.

———. *L'Invention de l'exégèse moderne: Les «Livres de Moïse» de 1650 à 1750*. Paris: Cerf, 2003.

———. *Petite histoire de l'exégèse biblique: De la lecture allégorique à l'exégèse critique*. Paris: Cerf, 1992.

Gillespie, Michael Allen. *The Theological Origins of Modernity*. Chicago: University of Chicago Press, 2008.

Gordon, Walter J. "The Monastic Achievement and More's Utopian Dream." *Medievalia et Humanistica* 9 (1979) 199–214.

Goshen-Gottstein, M. H. "Christianity, Judaism and Modern Bible Study." In *Congress Volume: Edinburgh 1974*, 69–88. Leiden: Brill, 1975.

———. "Foundations of Biblical Philology in the Seventeenth Century: Christian and Jewish Dimensions." In *Jewish Thought in the Seventeenth Century*, edited by Isadore Twersky and Bernard Septimus, 77–94. Cambridge: Harvard University Press, 1987.

———. "The Revival of Hebraic Studies as Part of the Humanist Revival Around 1500." *Hebrew University Studies in Literature and the Arts* 16 (1988) 185–91.

———. "The Textual Criticism of the Old Testament: Rise, Decline, Rebirth." *Journal of Biblical Literature* 102 (1983) 365–99.

Grafton, Anthony T. *Defenders of the Text: The Traditions of Scholarship in an Age of Science, 1450–1800*. Cambridge: Harvard University Press, 1991.

———. *Joseph Scaliger: A Study in the History of Classical Scholarship*. Vol 1, *Textual Criticism and Exegesis*. Oxford: Clarendon, 1983.

———. *Joseph Scaliger: A Study in the History of Classical Scholarship*. Vol. 2, *Historical Chronology*. Oxford: Clarendon, 1993.

———. "*Prolegomena* to Friedrich August Wolf." *Journal of the Warburg and Courtauld Institutes* 44 (1981) 101–29.

Greenspoon, Leonard. *Max Leopold Margolis: A Scholar's Scholar*. Atlanta: Scholars Press, 1987.

Gregory, Brad S. *The Unintended Reformation: How a Religious Revolution Secularized Society*. Cambridge: Harvard University Press, 2012.

Gross, Michael B. *The War Against Catholicism: Liberalism and the Anti-Catholic Imagination in Nineteenth-Century Germany*. Ann Arbor: University of Michigan Press, 2004.

Hadley, Judith M. "William Robertson Smith and the Asherah." In *William Robertson Smith: Essays in Reassessment*, edited by William Johnstone, 164–79. Sheffield: Sheffield Academic, 1995.

Hahn, Scott W. "At the School of Truth: The Ecclesial Character of Theology and Exegesis in the Thought of Benedict XVI." In *The Bible and the University*, edited by David Lyle Jeffrey and C. Stephen Evans, 80–115. Grand Rapids: Zondervan, 2007.

———. "The Authority of Mystery: The Biblical Theology of Benedict XVI." *Letter & Spirit* 2 (2006) 97–140.

———. *Covenant and Communion: The Biblical Theology of Pope Benedict XVI*. Grand Rapids: Brazos, 2009.

———. "The Hermeneutic of Faith: Pope Benedict XVI on Scripture, Liturgy, and Church." *The Incarnate Word* 1.3 (2007) 415–40.

———. *Kinship by Covenant: A Canonical Approach to the Fulfillment of God's Saving Promises*. New Haven: Yale University Press, 2009.

Hahn, Scott W., and Benjamin Wiker. *Politicizing the Bible: The Roots of Historical Criticism and the Secularization of Scripture 1300–1700*. New York: Herder & Herder, 2013.

Halpern, Baruch. *The First Historians: The Hebrew Bible and History*. University Park: Pennsylvania State University Press, 1996 (1988).

Hammill, Graham. *The Mosaic Constitution: Political Theology and Imagination from Machiavelli to Milton*. Chicago: University of Chicago Press, 2012.

Harrisville, Roy A., and Walter Sundberg. *The Bible in Modern Culture: Baruch Spinoza to Brevard Childs*. Grand Rapids: Eerdmans, 1995.

Hauerwas, Stanley. *The State of the University: Academic Knowledges and the Knowledge of God*. Malden, MA: Blackwell, 2007.

Hayes, John H. "Wellhausen as a Historian of Israel." *Semeia* 25 (1982) 37–60.

Hazard, Paul. *La crise de la conscience européenne, 1680–1715*. Paris: Boivin et Cie, 1935.

Helmholz, R. H. "Natural Law and the Trial of Thomas More." In *Thomas More's Trial by Jury: A Procedural and Legal Review with a Collection of Documents*, edited by Henry Ansgar Kelly, Louis W. Karlin, and Gerard B. Wegemer, 53–70. Woodbridge, England: Boydell, 2011.

Hess, Jonathan M. "Johann David Michaelis and the Colonial Imaginary: Orientalism and the Emergence of Racial Antisemitism in Eighteenth-Century Germany." *Jewish Social Studies* 6.2 (2000) 56–101.

Hexter, J. H. "Introduction: Part I." In *The Complete Works of St. Thomas More*. Vol. 4, *Utopia*, edited by Edward Surtz, S.J., and J. H. Hexter, xlv–cv. New Haven: Yale University Press, 1965.

Hornig, Gottfried. *Johann Salomo Semler: Studien zu Leben und Werk des Hallenser Aufklärungstheologen*. Tübingen: Niemeyer, 1996.

Howard, Thomas Albert. *Religion and the Rise of Historicism: W.M.L. de Wette, Jacob Burckhardt, and the Theological Origins of Nineteenth-Century Historical Consciousness*. Cambridge: Cambridge University Press, 2000.

Hunter, Alastair G. "The Indemnity: William Robertson Smith and George Adam Smith." In *William Robertson Smith: Essays in Reassessment*, edited by William Johnstone, 60–66. Sheffield: Sheffield Academic, 1995.

Hunter, Ian. "Multiple Enlightenments: Rival *Aufklärer* at the University of Halle, 1690–1730." In *The Enlightenment World*, edited by Martin Fitzpatrick, Peter Jones, Christa Knellwolf, and Iain McCalman, 576–95. London: Routledge, 2007.

Iofrida, Manlio. "The Original Lost: Writing and History in the Works of Richard Simon." *Topoi* 7 (1988) 211–19.

James, Susan. *Spinoza on Philosophy, Religion, and Politics: The Theologico-Political Treatise*. Oxford: Oxford University Press, 2012.

Jarick, John, ed. *Sacred Conjectures: The Context and Legacy of Robert Lowth and Jean Astruc*. London: T. & T. Clark, 2007.

Jindo, Job Y. "Revisiting Kaufmann: Fundamental Problems in Modern Biblical Scholarship." *Journal of the Interdisciplinary Study of Monotheistic Religions* 3 (2007) 41–77.

Jodock, Darrell. "Introduction II: The Modernists and the Anti-Modernists." In *Catholicism Contending with Modernity: Roman Catholic Modernism and Anti-Modernism in Historical Context*, edited by Darrell Jodock, 20–27. Cambridge: Cambridge University Press, 2000.

John Paul II, Pope. "Fides et Ratio." *Acta Apostolicae Sedis* 91 (1999) 5–88.

———. *Veritatis Splendor*. Vatican City: Libreria Editrice Vaticana, 1993.

Johnson, Luke Timothy. "What's Catholic About Catholic Biblical Scholarship?" In *The Future of Catholic Biblical Scholarship: A Constructive Conversation*, edited by Luke Timothy Johnson and William S. Kurz, S.J., 3–34. Grand Rapids: Eerdmans, 2002.

Johnstone, Willliam. "The Legacy of William Robertson Smith: Reading the Hebrew Bible with Arabic-Sensitized Eyes." In *William Robertson Smith: Essays in Reassessment*, edited by William Johnstone, 390–97. Sheffield: Sheffield Academic, 1995.

———, ed. *William Robertson Smith: Essays in Reassessment*. Sheffield: Sheffield Academic, 1995.

Jonas, Hans. *The Gnostic Religion: The Message of the Alien God and the Beginnings of Christianity*. 3rd ed. Boston: Beacon, 2001.

Jones, Andrew Willard. *Before Church and State: A Study of Social Order in the Sacramental Kingdom of St. Louis IX*. Steubenville: Emmaus Academic, 2017.

Jorink, Eric. "'Horrible and Blasphemous': Isaac La Peyrère, Isaac Vossius and the Emergence of Radical Biblical Criticism in the Dutch Republic." In vol. 1 of *Nature and Scripture in the Abrahamic Religions: Up to 1700*, edited by Jitse M. van der Meer and Scott Mandelbrote, 429–550. Leiden: Bril, 2008.

Kaplan, Yosef. "The Social Functions of the *Herem* in the Portuguese Jewish Community of Amsterdam in the Seventeenth Century." In vol. 1 of *Dutch Jewish History*, edited by Jozeph Michman and Tirtsah Levie, 111–55. Jerusalem: Tel-Aviv University, 1984.

Karlin, Louis W., and David R. Oakley. "A Guide to Thomas More's Trial for Modern Lawyers." In *Thomas More's Trial by Jury: A Procedural and Legal Review with a Collection of Documents*, edited by Henry Ansgar Kelly, Louis W. Karlin, and Gerard B. Wegemer, 71–93. Woodbridge, England: Boydell, 2011.

Karlin, Louis W., et al. "Judicial Commentary on Thomas More's Trial: Round Table." In *Thomas More's Trial by Jury: A Procedural and Legal Review with a Collection of Documents*, edited by Henry Ansgar Kelly, Louis W. Karlin, and Gerard B. Wegemer, 119–35. Woodbridge, England: Boydell, 2011.

Katchen, Aaron L. *Christian Hebraists and Dutch Rabbis: Seventeenth Century Apologetics and the Study of Maimonides' Mishneh Torah*. Cambridge: Harvard University Center for Jewish Studies, 1984.

Keenan, James F. *A History of Catholic Moral Theology in the Twentieth Century: From Confessing Sins to Liberating Consciences*. New York: Continuum, 2010.

Kelly, Henry Ansgar. "A Procedural Review of Thomas More's Trial." In *Thomas More's Trial by Jury: A Procedural and Legal Review with a Collection of Documents*, edited by Henry Ansgar Kelly, Louis W. Karlin, and Gerard B. Wegemer, 1–52. Woodbridge: Boydell, 2011.

Kelly, Henry Ansgar, Louis W. Karlin, and Gerard B. Wegemer. Preface to *Thomas More's Trial by Jury: A Procedural and Legal Review with a Collection of Documents*, edited by Henry Ansgar Kelly, Louis W. Karlin, and Gerard B. Wegemer, xi–xvii. Woodbridge, England: Boydell, 2011.

Kinnear, Malcolm A. "William Robertson Smith and the Death of Christ." In *William Robertson Smith: Essays in Reassessment*, edited by William Johnstone, 95–100. Sheffield: Sheffield Academic, 1995.

Kinney, Daniel, ed. *The Complete Works of St. Thomas More*. Vol. 15, *In Defense of Humanism: Letter to Martin Dorp, Letter to the University of Oxford, Letter to Edward Lee, and Letter to a Monk, with a New Text and Translation of Historia Richard Tertii*. New Haven: Yale University Press, 1986.

————. Introduction to *The Complete Works of St. Thomas More*. Vol. 15: *In Defense of Humanism: Letter to Martin Dorp, Letter to the University of Oxford, Letter to Edward Lee, and Letter to a Monk, with a New Text and Translation of Historia Richard Tertii*, edited by Daniel Kinney, xvii–xcii. New Haven: Yale University Press, 1986.

Klijnsmit, A. J. "Some Seventeenth-Century Grammatical Descriptions of Hebrew." *Histoire Épistémologie Langage* 12.1 (1990) 77–101.

————. "Spinoza and the Grammarians of the Bible." In *The History of Linguistics in the Low Countries*, edited by Jan Noordegraaf, Kees Versteegh, and E. F. K. Koerner, 155–200. Amsterdam: John Benjamins, 1992.

————. *Spinoza and Grammatical Tradition*. Leiden: Brill, 1986.

Knight, Douglas A. *Rediscovering the Traditions of Israel*. 3rd rev. ed. Atlanta: Society of Biblical Literature, 2006.

————. "Wellhausen and the Interpretation of Israel's Literature." *Semeia* 25 (1982) 21–36.

Kratz, Reinhard G. "Eyes and Spectacles: Wellhausen's Method of Higher Criticism." *Journal of Theological Studies* 60 (2009) 381–402.

Kraus, Hans-Joachim. *Geschichte der historisch-kritischen Erforschung des Alten Testaments*. Kreis Moers: Neukirchener, 1956.

Kristeller, Paul Oskar. "Thomas More as a Renaissance Humanist." *Moreana* 65–66 (1980) 5–22.

Kugel, James L. "The Bible in the University." In *The Hebrew Bible and Its Interpreters*, edited by William Henry Propp, Baruch Halpern, and David Noel Freedman, 143–65. Winona Lake, IN: Eisenbrauns, 1990.

————. *How to Read the Bible: A Guide to Scripture, Then and Now*. New York: Free Press, 2007.

Laplanche, François. *L'écriture, le sacré et l'histoire: Érudits et politiques protestants devant la Bible en France au XVIIe siècle.* Amsterdam: Holland University Press, 1986.

Lazarus-Yafeh, Hava. *Intertwined Worlds: Medieval Islam and Bible Criticism.* Princeton: Princeton University Press, 1992.

Lease, Gary. "Vatican Foreign Policy and the Origins of Modernism." In *Catholicism Contending with Modernity: Roman Catholic Modernism and Anti-Modernism in Historical Context,* edited by Darrell Jodock, 31–55. Cambridge: Cambridge University Press, 2000.

Legaspi, Michael C. *The Death of Scripture and the Rise of Biblical Studies.* Oxford: Oxford University Press, 2010.

Levenson, Jon D. *The Hebrew Bible, the Old Testament, and Historical Criticism: Jews and Christians in Biblical Studies.* Louisville: Westminster John Knox, 1993.

Levering, Matthew. *Biblical Natural Law: A Theocentric and Teleological Approach.* Oxford: Oxford University Press, 2008.

Levy, Ian Christopher. *Holy Scripture and the Quest for Authority at the End of the Middle Ages.* Notre Dame: Univeristy of Notre Dame Press, 2012.

Lorberbaum, Menachem. "Spinoza's Theological-Political Problem." In *Political Hebraism: Judaic Sources in Early Modern Political Thought,* edited by Gordon Schochet, Fania Oz-Salzberger, and Meirav Jones, 167–88. Jerusalem: Shalem, 2008.

Lutzky, Harriet. "Deity and Social Bond: Robertson Smith and the Psychoanalytic Theory of Religion." In *William Robertson Smith: Essays in Reassessment,* edited by William Johnstone, 320–30. Sheffield: Sheffield Academic, 1995.

Lynch, Christopher. "Machiavelli on Reading the Bible Judiciously." In *Political Hebraism: Judaic Sources in Early Modern Political Thought,* edited by Gordon Schochet, Fania Oz-Salzberger, and Meirav Jones, 29–54. Jerusalem: Shalem, 2008.

Lynch, John J. "Notes on Moral Theology." *Theological Studies* 19.2 (1958) 165–98.

Machinist, Peter. "The Road Not Taken: Wellhausen and Assyriology." In *Homeland and Exile: Biblical and Ancient Near Eastern Studies in Honour of Bustenay Oded,* edited by Gershon Galil, Mark Geller, and Alan Millard, 469–531. Leiden: Brill, 2009.

Maier, Bernhard. *William Robertson Smith: His Life, His Work and His Times.* Tübingen: Mohr Siebeck, 2009.

Malcolm, Noel. *Aspects of Hobbes.* Oxford: Oxford University Press, 2002.

Manrique Charry, Juan Francisco. "La herencia de Bacon en la doctrina spinocista del lenguaje." *Universitas Philosophica* 54 (2010) 121–30.

Manuel, Frank E. *The Broken Staff: Judaism through Christian Eyes.* Cambridge: Harvard University Press, 1992.

Marc'hadour, Germain. *The Bible in the Works of St. Thomas More.* Part 1, *The Old Testament.* Nieuwkoop: B. de Graaf, 1969.

———. *The Bible in the Works of St. Thomas More.* Part 2, *The Four Gospels.* Nieuwkoop: B. de Graaf, 1969.

———. *The Bible in the Works of St. Thomas More.* Part 3, *Acts, Epistles, Apocalypse.* Nieuwkoop: B. de Graaf, 1970.

———. *The Bible in the Works of St. Thomas More.* Part 4, *Elements of Synthesis.* Nieuwkoop: B. de Graaf, 1971.

———. *The Bible in the Works of St. Thomas More*. Part 5, *Indexes, Supplements, Concordances*. Nieuwkoop: B. de Graaf, 1972.

———. "Scripture in the Dialogue." In *The Complete Works of St. Thomas More*. Vol. 6, *A Dialogue Concerning Heresies*, Part 2, *Introduction and Commentary*, edited by Thomas M. C. Lawler, Germain Marc'hadour, and Richard C. Marius, 494–526. New Haven: Yale University Press, 1981.

———. *Thomas More et la Bible: La place des livres saints dans son apologétique et sa spiritualité*. Paris: J. Vrin, 1969.

Marchand, Suzanne L. *Down from Olympus: Archaeology and Philhellenism in Germany, 1750–1970*. Princeton: Princeton University Press, 1996.

———. *German Orientalism in the Age of Empire: Religion, Race, and Scholarship*. Cambridge: Cambridge University Press, 2010.

Marshall, Peter. "The Last Years." In *The Cambridge Companion to Thomas More*, edited by George M. Logan, 116–38. Cambridge: Cambridge University Press, 2011.

Marx, Steven. "Moses and Machiavellism." *Journal of the American Academy of Religion* 65.3 (1997) 551–71.

Masuzawa, Tomoko. *The Invention of World Religions: Or, How European Universalism was Preserved in the Language of Pluralism*. Chicago: University of Chicago Press, 2005.

McConica, James. "Thomas More as Humanist." In *The Cambridge Companion to Thomas More*, edited by George M. Logan, 22–45. Cambridge: Cambridge University Press, 2011.

McCutcheon, Elizabeth. "More's Rhetoric." In *The Cambridge Companion to Thomas More*, edited by George M. Logan, 46–68. Cambridge: Cambridge University Press, 2011.

———. "Thomas More's Three Prison Letters Reporting on His Interrogations." In *Thomas More's Trial by Jury: A Procedural and Legal Review with a Collection of Documents*, edited by Henry Ansgar Kelly, Louis W. Karlin, and Gerard B. Wegemer, 94–110. Woodbridge: Boydell, 2011.

McGreevy, John T. *Catholicism and American Freedom: A History*. New York: Norton, 2003.

McKane, William. *Selected Christian Hebraists*. Cambridge: Cambridge University Press, 1989.

Meeks, Wayne A. "A Nazi New Testament Professor Reads the Bible: The Strange Case of Gerhard Kittel." In *The Idea of Biblical Interpretation: Essays in Honor of James L. Kugel*, edited by H. Najman and J. H. Newman, 513–44. Leiden: Brill, 2004.

Milbank, John. *Theology and Social Theory: Beyond Secular Reason*. 2nd ed. Malden: Blackwell, 2006.

Miller, Patrick D. "Wellhausen and the History of Israel's Religion." *Semeia* 25 (1982) 61–73.

Minnis, A. J. "Material Swords and Literal Lights: The Status of Allegory in William of Ockham's *Breviloquium* on Papal Power." In *With Reverence for the Word: Medieval Scriptural Exegesis in Judaism, Christianity, and Islam*, edited by Jane Dammen McAuliffe, Barry D. Walfish, and Joseph W. Goering, 292–308. Oxford: Oxford University Press, 2003.

Mirri, F. Saverio. *Richard Simon e il metodo storico-critico di B. Spinoza. Storia di un libro e di una polemica sulla sfondo delle lotte politico-religiose della Francia di Luigi XIV*. Florence: Le Monnier, 1972.

Mittleman, Alan. "Some Thoughts on the Covenantal Politics of Johannes Althusius." In *Political Hebraism: Judaic Sources in Early Modern Political Thought*, edited by Gordon Schochet, Fania Oz-Salzberger, and Meirav Jones, 72–89. Jerusalem: Shalem, 2008.

Momigliano, Arnaldo. "La nuova storia romana di G.B. Vico." *Rivista storica italiana* 77 (1965) 773–90.

———. "Religious History Without Frontiers: J. Wellhausen, U. Wilamowitz, and E. Schwartz." *History and Theory* 21.4 (1982) 49–64.

Moorman, Mary C. *Indulgences: Luther, Catholicism, and the Imputation of Merit.* Steubenville: Emmaus Academic, forthcoming 2017.

Morales, José. "La formación espiritual e intelectual de Tomás Moro y sus contactos con la doctrina y obras de Santo Tomás de Aquino." *Scripta Theologica* 6 (1974) 439–89.

Morrison, John. "William Robertson Smith and the Academy of Old Deer." In *William Robertson Smith: Essays in Reassessment*, edited by William Johnstone, 50–59. Sheffield: Sheffield Academic, 1995.

Morrow, Jeffrey L. "The Acid of History: La Peyrère, Hobbes, Spinoza, and the Separation of Faith and Reason in Modern Biblical Studies." *Heythrop Journal* (forthcoming).

———. "Alfred Loisy and les Mythes Babyloniens: Loisy's Discourse on Myth in the Context of Modernism." *Journal for the History of Modern Theology/Zeitschrift für Neuere Theologiegeschichte* 21.1 (2014) 87–103.

———. "Alfred Loisy's Developmental Approach to Scripture: Reading the 'Firmin' Articles in the Context of Nineteenth- and Twentieth-Century Historical Biblical Criticism." *International Journal of Systematic Theology* 15 (2013) 324–44.

———. "Averroism, Nominalism, and Mechanization: Hahn and Wiker's Unmasking of Historical Criticism's Political Agenda by Laying Bare its Philosophical Roots." *Nova et Vetera* 14.4 (2016) 1293–1340.

———. "Babylon in Paris: Alfred Loisy as Assyriologist." *Journal of Religious History* 40.2 (2016) 261–76.

———. "Babylonian Myths and the Bible: The Historical and Religious Context to Loisy's Application of 'Myth' as a Concept." *Papers of the Nineteenth Century Theology Group* 44 (2013) 43–62.

———. "The Bible in Captivity: Hobbes, Spinoza and the Politics of Defining Religion." *Pro Ecclesia* 19.3 (2010) 285–99.

———. "Cut Off from Its Wellspring: The Politics Behind the Divorce of Scripture from Catholic Moral Theology." *Heythrop Journal* 56.4 (2015) 547–58.

———. "*Dei Verbum* in Light of the History of Catholic Biblical Interpretation." *Josephinum Journal of Theology* (forthcoming).

———. "The Early Modern Political Context to Spinoza's Bible Criticism." *Revista de Filosofía* 66.3 (2010) 7–24.

———. "The Enlightenment University and the Creation of the Academic Bible: Michael Legaspi's *The Death of Scripture and the Rise of Biblical Studies.*" *Nova et Vetera* 11.3 (2013) 897–922.

———. "*Études Assyriologie* and 19th and 20th Century French Historical-Biblical Criticism." *Near Eastern Archaeological Society Bulletin* 59 (2014) 3–20.

———. "Faith, Reason and History in Early Modern Catholic Biblical Interpretation: Fr. Richard Simon and St. Thomas More." *New Blackfriars* 96 (2015) 658–73.

———. "The Fate of Catholic Biblical Interpretation in America." In *Sources of American Catholicism: Essays in Honor of William L. Portier*, edited by Timothy Gabrielli and Derek Hatch. Eugene: Pickwick, forthcoming.

———. "French Apocalyptic Messianism: Isaac La Peyrère and Political Biblical Criticism in the Seventeenth Century." *Toronto Journal of Theology* 27.2 (2011) 203–13.

———. "Historical Criticism as Secular Allegorism: The Case of Spinoza." *Letter & Spirit* 8 (2013) 189–221.

———. "*Leviathan* and the Swallowing of Scripture: The Politics behind Thomas Hobbes' Early Modern Biblical Criticism." *Christianity & Literature* 61.1 (2011) 33–54.

———. "Loisy, Alfred Firmin." In *Encyclopedia of the Bible and Its Reception, Volume H*, edited by Hans-Josef Klauck, et al. Berlin: Walter de Gruyter, forthcoming.

———. "The Modernist Crisis and the Shifting of Catholic Views on Biblical Inspiration." *Letter & Spirit* 6 (2010) 265–80.

———. "The Politics of Biblical Interpretation: A 'Criticism of Criticism.'" *New Blackfriars* 91 (2010) 528–45.

———. "Pre-Adamites, Politics and Criticism: Isaac La Peyrère's Contribution to Modern Biblical Studies." *Journal of the Orthodox Center for the Advancement of Biblical Studies* 4.1 (2011) 1–23.

———. "Secularization, Objectivity, and Enlightenment Scholarship: The Theological and Political Origins of Modern Biblical Studies." *Logos* 18.1 (2015) 14–32.

———. "Spinoza and Modern Biblical Hermeneutics: The Theo-Political Implications of His Freedom to Philosophize." *New Blackfriars* (forthcoming).

———. "Spinoza's Use of the Psalms in the Context of His Political Project." *Interdisciplinary Journal of Research on Religion* 11 (2015) 1–18.

———. "St. Thomas More on the Sadness of Christ: From Mystagogy to Martyrdom." *Heythrop Journal* (forthcoming).

———. *Three Skeptics and the Bible: La Peyrère, Hobbes, Spinoza, and the Reception of Modern Biblical Criticism*. Eugene, OR: Pickwick, 2016.

———. "The Untold History of Modern Biblical Scholarship's Pre-Enlightenment Secular Origins." *Journal of Theological Interpretation* 8.1 (2014) 145–55.

Müller, Sascha. "Grammatik und Wahrheit. Salomon Glassius (1593–1656) und Richard Simon (1638–1712) im Gespräch." In *Hebraistik—Hermenteutik—Homiletik: Die 'Philologia Sacra' im frühneuzeitlichen Bibelstudium*, edited by Christoph Bultmann and Lutz Danneberg, 515–33. Berlin: de Gruyter, 2011.

———. *Kritik und Theologie: Christliche Glaubens und Schrifthermeneutik nach Richard Simon*. St. Ottilien: EOS, 2004.

———. *Richard Simon (1638–1712): Exeget, Theologe, Philosoph und Historiker*. Bamberg: Echter, 2006.

Nadler, Steven. *A Book Forged in Hell: Spinoza's Scandalous Treatise and the Birth of the Secular Age*. Princeton: Princeton University Press, 2011.

Nahkola, Aulikki. *Double Narratives in the Old Testament: The Foundations of Method in Biblical Criticism*. Berlin: de Gruyter, 2001.

Nelson, Eric. *The Hebrew Republic: Jewish Sources and the Transformation of European Political Thought*. Cambridge: Harvard University Press, 2010.

Neuman, Kalman. "Political Hebraism and the Early Modern 'Respublica Hebraeorum': On Defining the Field." In *Political Hebraism: Judaic Sources in Early Modern*

Political Thought, edited by Gordon Schochet, Fania Oz-Salzberger, and Meirav Jones, 57–70. Jerusalem: Shalem, 2008.

Nichols, Francis W. "Richard Simon: Faith and Modernity." In *Christianity and the Stranger: Historical Essays*, edited by Francis W. Nichols, 115–68. Atlanta: Scholars Press, 1995.

Novick, Peter. *That Noble Dream: The "Objectivity Question" and the American Historical Profession*. Cambridge: Cambridge University Press, 1988.

Oberman, Heiko A. *The Dawn of the Reformation: Essays in Late Medieval and Early Reformation Thought*. Grand Rapids: Eerdmans, 1992.

———. *The Harvest of Medieval Theology*. Cambridge: Harvard University Press, 1963.

———. *Masters of the Reformation: The Emergence of a New Intellectual Climate in Europe*. Cambridge: Cambridge University Press, 1981.

O'Connell, Marvin R. *Critics on Trial: An Introduction to the Catholic Modernist Crisis*. Washington, DC: The Catholic University of America, 1994.

O'Neill, J. C. "Adolf von Harnack and the Entry of the German State into War, July–August 1914." *Scottish Journal of Theology* 55 (2002) 1–18.

———. *The Bible's Authority: A Portrait Gallery of Thinkers from Lessing to Bultmann*. London: T. & T. Clark, 1991.

Osier, Jean Pierre. "L'herméneutique de Hobbes et de Spinoza." *Studia Spinozana* 3 (1987) 319–47.

Oz-Salzberger, Fania. "The Political Thought of John Locke and the Significance of Political Hebraism: Then and Now." In *Political Hebraism: Judaic Sources in Early Modern Political Thought*, edited by Gordon Schochet, Fania Oz-Salzberger, and Meirav Jones, 231–56. Jerusalem: Shalem, 2008.

Pacchi, Arrigo. "Hobbes and Biblical Philology in the Service of the State." *Topoi* 7.3 (1988) 231–39.

———. "Hobbes e l'epicureismo." *Rivista critica di storia della filosofia* 33 (1975) 54–71.

———. "*Leviathan* and Spinoza's *Tractatus* on Revelation: Some Elements for a Comparison." *History of European Ideas* 10 (1989) 577–93.

Parkin, Jon. "The Reception of Hobbes's *Leviathan*." In *The Cambridge Companion to Hobbes's Leviathan*, edited by Patricia Springborg, 441–59. Cambridge: Cambridge University Press, 2007.

Parman, Susan. "William Robertson Smith and American Anthropology: Science, Religion, and Interpretation." In *William Robertson Smith: Essays in Reassessment*, edited by William Johnstone, 264–71. Sheffield: Sheffield Academic, 1995.

Pasto, James. "Islam's 'Strange Secret Sharer': Orientalism, Judaism, and the Jewish Question." *Comparative Studies in Society and History* 40.3 (1998) 437–74.

———. "When the End Is the Beginning? Or When the Biblical Past Is the Political Present: Some Thoughts on Ancient Israel, 'Post-Exilic Judaism,' and the Politics of Biblical Scholarship." *Scandinavian Journal of the Old Testament* 1.2 (1998) 157–202.

———. "W. M. L. de Wette and the Invention of Post-Exilic Judaism: Political Historiography and Christian Allegory in Nineteenth-Century German Biblical Scholarship." In *Jews, Antiquity, and the Nineteenth-Century Imagination*, edited by Hayim Lapin and Dale Marin, 33–52. Bethesda, MD: University Press of Maryland, 2003.

Perreau-Saussine, Emile. "Why Draw a Politics from Scripture? Bossuet and the Divine Right of Kings." In *Political Hebraism: Judaic Sources in Early Modern Political*

Thought, edited by Gordon Schochet, Fania Oz-Salzberger, and Meirav Jones, 90–104. Jerusalem: Shalem, 2008.

Philsooph, Hushang. "A Reconsideration of Frazer's Relationship with Robertson Smith: The Myth and the Facts." In *William Robertson Smith: Essays in Reassessment,* edited by William Johnstone, 331–42. Sheffield: Sheffield Academic, 1995.

Pietsch, Andreas Nikolaus. *Isaac La Peyrère: Bibelkritik, Philosemitismus und Patronage in der Gelehrtenrepublik des 17. Jahrhunderts.* Berlin: de Gruyter, 2012.

Pinckaers, Servais. "Scripture and the Renewal of Moral Theology." In *The Pinckaers Reader: Renewing Thomistic Moral Theology,* edited by John Berkman and Craig Steven Titus, 46–63. Washington, DC: The Catholic University of America Press, 2005.

———. *The Sources of Christian Ethics.* Washington, DC: The Catholic University of America Press, 1995.

Popkin, Richard H. "Bible Criticism and Social Science." In *Methodological and Historical Essays in the Natural and Social Sciences,* edited by Robert S. Cohen and Marx W. Wartofsky, 339–60. Dordrecht: Reidel, 1974.

———. "The Development of Religious Scepticism and the Influence of Isaac La Peyrère's Pre-Adamism and Bible Criticism." In *Classical Influences on European Culture, AD 1500–1700,* edited by Robert Ralf Bolgar, 271–80. Cambridge: Cambridge University Press, 1976.

———. "Hume and Spinoza." *Hume Studies* 5 (1979) 65–93.

———. *Isaac La Peyrère (1596–1676): His Life, Work and Influence.* Leiden: Brill, 1987.

———. "Millenarianism and Nationalism—A Case Study: Isaac La Peyrère." In *Millenarianism and Messianism in Early Modern European Culture.* Vol. 4, *Continental Millenarians: Protestants, Catholics, Heretics,* edited by John Christian Laursen and Richard H. Popkin, 74–84. Dordrecht: Kluwer Academic, 2001.

———. "Some New Light on the Roots of Spinoza's Science of Bible Study." In *Spinoza and the Sciences,* edited by Margorie Grene and Debora Nails, 171–88. Dordrecht: Kluwer Academic, 1986.

———. *Spinoza.* Oxford: Oneworld, 2004.

———. "Spinoza and La Peyrère." *Southwestern Journal of Philosophy* 3 (1977) 172–95.

———. "Spinoza, the Quakers and the Millenarians, 1656–1658." *Manuscrito* 6 (1982) 113–33.

———. "Spinoza and Samuel Fisher." *Philosophia* 15 (1985) 219–36.

———. "Spinoza's Relations with the Quakers in Amsterdam." *Quaker History* 73 (1984) 14–28.

Portier, William L. "Church Unity and National Traditions: The Challenge to the Modern Papacy, 1682–1870." In *The Papacy and the Church in the United States,* edited by Bernard Cooke, 25–54. New York: Paulist, 1989.

———. *Divided Friends: Portraits of the Roman Catholic Modernist Crisis in the United States.* Washington, DC: The Catholic University of America Press, 2013.

Powers, David S. "Reading/Misreading One Another's Scriptures: Ibn Ḥazm's Refutation of Ibn Nagrella al-Yahū d ī." In *Studies in Islamic and Judaic Traditions: Papers Presented at the Institute for Islamic-Judaic Studies,* edited by William M. Brinner and Stephen D. Ricks, 109–21. Atlanta: Scholars Press, 1986.

Preus, J. Samuel. *Spinoza and the Irrelevance of Biblical Authority.* Cambridge: Cambridge University Press, 2001.

Räisänen, Heikki. *Marcion, Muhammad and the Mahatma: Exegetical Perspectives on the Encounter of Cultures and Faith*. London: SCM, 1997.

Raurell, Federic. "Mètode d'aproximació de la Bíblia en el *Jesús de Natzaret* de Joseph Ratzinger/Benet XVI." *Revista Catalana de Teologia* 32.2 (2007) 435–58.

Reif, Stefan C. "William Robertson Smith in Relation to Hebraists and Jews at Christ's College Cambridge." In *William Robertson Smith: Essays in Reassessment*, edited by William Johnstone, 210–23. Sheffield: Sheffield Academic, 1995.

Reiser, Marius. *Bibelkritik und Auslegung der Heiligen Schrift*. Tübingen: Mohr Siebeck, 2007.

Remer, Gary. "After Machiavelli and Hobbes: James Harrington's Commonwealth of Israel." In *Political Hebraism: Judaic Sources in Early Modern Political Thought*, edited by Gordon Schochet, Fania Oz-Salzberger, and Meirav Jones, 207–30. Jerusalem: Shalem, 2008.

Rendtorff, Rolf. "Die Hebräische Bibel als Grundlage christlich-theologischer Aussagen über das Judentum." In *Jüdische Existenz und die Erneuerung der christlichen Theologie. Versuch einer Bilanz des christlich-jüdischen Dialogs für die Systematische Theologie*, edited by Martin Stöhr, 32–47. Munich: Kaiser, 1981.

Reventlow, Henning Graf. *The Authority of the Bible and the Rise of the Modern World*. London: SCM, 1984.

———. *Bibelautorität und Geist der Moderne, Die bedeutung des Bibelverständnisses für die geistesgeschichtliche und politische Entwicklung in England von der Reformation bis zur Aufklärung*. Göttingen: Vandenhoeck & Ruprecht, 1980.

———. *Epochen der Bibelauslegung 4. Von der Aufklärung bis zum 20. Jahrhundert*. Munich: Beck, 2001.

———. *History of Biblical Interpretation*. Vol. 4, *From the Enlightenment to the Twentieth Century*. Atlanta: Society of Biblical Literature, 2010.

———. "Richard Simon und seine Bedeutung für die kritische Erforschung der Bibel." In *Historische Kritik in der Theologie*, edited by Georg Schwaiger, 11–36. Göttingen: Vandenhoeck & Ruprecht, 1980.

Reventlow, Henning Graf, Walter Sparn, and John Woodbridge, eds. *Historische Kritik und biblischer Kanon in der deutschen Aufklärung*. Wiesbaden: Harrossowtiz, 1988.

Reventlow, Henning Graf, and William Farmer, eds. *Biblical Studies and the Shifting of Paradigms, 1850–1914*. Sheffield: Sheffield Academic, 1995.

Rex, Richard. "Thomas More and the Heretics: Statesman or Fanatic?" In *The Cambridge Companion to Thomas More*, edited by George M. Logan, 93–115. Cambridge: Cambridge University Press, 2011.

Riesen, Richard Allan. "Scholarship and Piety: The Sermons of William Robertson Smith." In *William Robertson Smith: Essays in Reassessment*, edited by William Johnstone, 86–94. Sheffield: Sheffield Academic, 1995.

Rivière, Jean. *Le Modernisme dans l'église*. Paris: Letouzey, 1929.

Rivière, Peter. "William Robertson Smith and John Ferguson McLennan: The Aberdeen Roots of British Social Anthropology." In *William Robertson Smith: Essays in Reassessment*, edited by William Johnstone, 293–302. Sheffield: Sheffield Academic, 1995.

Rodgers, Katherine Gardiner. "The Lessons of Gethsemane: *De Tristitia Christi*." In *The Cambridge Companion to Thomas More*, edited by George M. Logan, 243–51. Cambridge: Cambridge University Press, 2011.

Rodrigues, M. A. "Algumas notas sobre o *Compendium Grammatices Hebraeae* de Baruch Spinoza." *Helmantica* 49 (1998) 111–29.

Rogerson, J. W. *The Bible and Criticism in Victorian England: Profiles of F. D. Maurice and William Robertson Smith.* Sheffield: Sheffield Academic, 1995.

———. *Old Testament Criticism in the Nineteenth Century: England and Germany.* London: SPCK, 1984.

———. *W.M.L. de Wette: Founder of Modern Biblical Criticism: An Intellectual Biography.* Sheffield: Sheffield Academic, 1992.

———. "W. R. Smith's *The Old Testament in the Jewish Church*: Its Antecedents, its Influence and its Abiding Value." In *William Robertson Smith: Essays in Reassessment*, edited by William Johnstone, 132–47. Sheffield: Sheffield Academic, 1995.

Rosenblatt, Jason. "Rabbinic Ideas in the Political Thought of John Seldon." In *Political Hebraism: Judaic Sources in Early Modern Political Thought*, edited by Gordon Schochet, Fania Oz-Salzberger, and Meirav Jones, 191–206. Jerusalem: Shalem, 2008.

Rosenthal, Michael A. "Miracles, Wonder, and the State." In *Spinoza's Theological-Political Treatise: A Critical Guide*, edited by Yitzhak Y. Melamed and Michael A. Rosenthal, 231–49. Cambridge: Cambridge University Press, 2010.

Rudolph, Kurt. "Wellhausen as an Arabist." *Semeia* 25 (1982) 111–55.

Sacksteder, William. "How Much of Hobbes Might Spinoza Have Read?" *Southwestern Journal of Philosophy* 11 (1980) 25–39.

Sæbø, Magne, ed. *Hebrew Bible/Old Testament: The History of Its Interpretation II: From the Renaissance to the Enlightenment.* Göttingen: Vandenhoeck & Ruprecht, 2008.

———. "Some Problems of Writing a Research History of Old Testament Studies in the Latter Part of the Nineteenth Century with Special Regard to the Life and Work of William Robertson Smith." In *William Robertson Smith: Essays in Reassessment*, edited by William Johnstone, 243–51. Sheffield: Sheffield Academic, 1995.

Sarna, Nahum M. "The Modern Study of the Bible in the Framework of Jewish Studies." *Proceedings of the Eighth World Congress of Jewish Studies* (1983) 19–27.

Schechter, Solomon. *Seminary Addresses and Other Papers.* Cincinnati: Ark, 1915.

Schmidt-Biggeman, Wilhelm. "Political Theology in Renaissance Christian Kabbala: Petrus Galatinus and Guillaume Postel." In *Political Hebraism: Judaic Sources in Early Modern Political Thought*, edited by Gordon Schochet, Fania Oz-Salzberger, and Meirav Jones, 3–28. Jerusalem: Shalem, 2008.

Schochet, Gordon. "The Judeo-Christian Tradition as Imposition: Present at the Creation?" In *Political Hebraism: Judaic Sources in Early Modern Political Thought*, edited by Gordon Schochet, Fania Oz-Salzberger, and Meirav Jones, 259–82. Jerusalem: Shalem, 2008.

Scholder, Klaus. *Ursprunge und Probleme der Bibelkritik im 17. Jahrhundert.* Munich: Kaiser, 1966.

Schönert, Jörg, and Friedrich Vollhardt, eds. *Geschichte der Hermeneutik und die Methodik der textinterpretierenden Disziplinen.* Berlin: Walter de Gruyter, 2005.

Schumann, Karl. "Methodenfragen bei Spinoza und Hobbes: Zum Problem des Einflusses." *Studia Spinozana* 3 (1987) 47–86.

Schwaiger, Georg, ed. *Historische Kritik in der Theologie: Beitrage zu ihrer Geschichte.* Göttingen: Vandenhoeck & Ruprecht, 1980.

Schwarzbach, Bertram Eugene. "The Eighteenth Century Confronts Job." *History of Universities* 22.1 (2007) 141–97.

———. "La fortune de Richard Simon au XVIIIe siècle." *Revue des études juives* 146 (1987) 225–39.

Scribner, R. W., and C. Scott Dixon. *The German Reformation*. 2nd ed. New York: Palgrave Macmillan, 2003.

Segal, Robert A. "Smith versus Frazer on the Comparative Method." In *William Robertson Smith: Essays in Reassessment*, edited by William Johnstone, 343–51. Sheffield: Sheffield Academic, 1995.

Sermoneta, Joseph B. "Biblical Anthropology in 'The Guide of the Perplexed' by Moses Maimonides, and its Reversal in the 'Tractatus theologico-politicus' by Baruch Spinoza." *Topoi* 7.3 (1988) 241–47.

Sheehan, Jonathan. *The Enlightenment Bible: Translation, Scholarship, Culture*. Princeton: Princeton University Press, 2005.

Shelford, April G. "Of Sceptres and Censors: Biblical Interpretation and Censorship in Seventeenth-Century France." *French History* 20 (2006) 161–81.

Shiel, Judith. "William Robertson Smith in the Nineteenth Century in the Light of His Correspondence." In *William Robertson Smith: Essays in Reassessment*, edited by William Johnstone, 78–85. Sheffield: Sheffield Academic, 1995.

Shuger, Debora Kuller. *The Renaissance Bible: Scholarship, Sacrifice, and Subjectivity*. Berkeley: University of California Press, 1994.

Siker, Jeffrey S. *Scripture in Ethics: Twentieth-Century Portraits*. Oxford: Oxford University Press, 1997.

Silberman, Lou H. "Wellhausen and Judaism." *Semeia* 25 (1982) 75–82.

Simon, Richard. *Histoire critique du Vieux Testament, suivi de Lettre sur l'inspiration: Nouvelle édition*. Edited by Pierre Gibert. Montrouge: Bayard, 2008.

Ska, Jean-Louis. "Richard Simon: Un pionnier sur les sentiers de la tradition." *Recherches de Science Religieuse* 97 (2009) 307–16.

Skinner, Quentin. *The Foundations of Modern Political Thought*. Vol. 2. Cambridge: Cambridge University Press, 1978.

Smend, Rudolf. *From Astruc to Zimmerli: Old Testament Scholarship in Three Centuries*. Tübingen: Mohr Siebeck, 2007.

———. "Julius Wellhausen and his *Prolegomena to the History of Israel*." *Semeia* 25 (1982) 1–20.

———. "William Robertson Smith and Julius Wellhausen." In *William Robertson Smith: Essays in Reassessment*, edited by William Johnstone, 226–42. Sheffield: Sheffield Academic, 1995.

Sörlin, Sverker. "National and International Aspects of Cross-Boundary Science: Scientific Travel in the 18th Century." In *Denationalizing Science: The Contexts of International Scientific Practice*, edited by Elisabeth Crawford, Terry Shinn, and Sverker Sörlin, 43–72. Dordrecht: Kluwer Academic, 1993.

———. "Ordering the World for Europe: Science as Intelligence and Information as Seen from the Northern Periphery." *Osiris* 15 (2000) 51–69.

Spinoza, Baruch. *Opera*. 4 vols. Edited by Carl Gebhardt. Heidelberg: Carl Winter, 1925.

———. *Theological-Political Treatise*. Edited by Jonathan Israel. Translated by Michael Silverthorne and Jonathan Israel. Cambridge: Cambridge University Press, 2007.

————. *Tractatus theologico-politicus/Traité théologico-politique*. Edited by Pierre-François Moreau. Translated and notes by Jacqueline Lagrée and Pierre-François Moreau. Paris: Presses Universitaires de France, 2012.

Springborg, Patricia. "Hobbes and Epicurean Religion." In *Der Garten und die Moderne: Epikureische Moral und Politik vom Humanismus bis zur Aufklärung*, edited by Gianni Paganini and Edoardo Tortarolo, 161–214. Stuttgart: Rommann-holzboog Verlag, 2004.

Steinmann, Jean. *Richard Simon et les origins de l'exégèse biblique*. Paris: Brouwer, 1960.

Stroumsa, Guy G. "Comparatisme et philologie: Richard Simon et la naissance de l'orientalisme." In *Le comparatisme en histoire des religions*, edited by François Bœspflug and François Dunand, 47–62. Paris: Cerf, 1997.

————. "Homeros Hebraios: Homère et la Bible aux origines de la culture européenne (17e–18e siècles)." In *L'orient dans l'histoire religieuse de l'europe: L'invention des origines*, edited by Mohammad Ali Amir-Moezzi and John Scheid, 87–100. Turnhout: Brepols, 2000.

————. "Jewish Myth and Ritual and the Beginnings of Comparative Religion: The Case of Richard Simon." *Journal of Jewish Thought and Philosophy* 6 (1997) 19–35.

————. "Richard Simon: From Philology to Comparatism." *Archiv für Religionsgeschichte* 3 (2001) 89–107.

Surtz, Edward. "Introduction: Part II." In *The Complete Works of St. Thomas More*. Vol. 4, *Utopia*, edited by Edward Surtz and J. H. Hexter, clvi–clxxix. New Haven: Yale University Press, 1965.

Talar, C. J. T. "Innovation and Biblical Interpretation." In *Catholicism Contending with Modernity: Roman Catholic Modernism and Anti-Modernism in Historical Context*, edited by Darrell Jodock, 191–211. Cambridge: Cambridge University Press, 2000.

————. *(Re)reading, Reception, and Rhetoric: Approaches to Roman Catholic Modernism*. New York: Peter Lang, 1999.

Tanner, Norman P., ed. *Decrees of the Ecumenical Councils*. Volume 2, *Trent to Vatican II*. Washington, DC: Georgetown University Press, 1990.

Thrower, James A. "Two Unlikely Travelling Companions: Sir Richard Burton and William Robertson Smith." In *William Robertson Smith: Essays in Reassessment*, edited by William Johnstone, 383–89. Sheffield: Sheffield Academic, 1995.

Tomes, F. Roger. "Samuel Davidson and William Robertson Smith: Parallel Cases?" In *William Robertson Smith: Essays in Reassessment*, edited by William Johnstone, 67–77. Sheffield: Sheffield Academic, 1995.

Tricaud, François. "L'Ancien Testament et le *Léviathan* de Hobbes: Une cohabitation difficile." *Rivista di Storia della Filosofia* 54.2 (1999) 229–38.

Tugendhat, Michael. "Judicial Commentary on Thomas More's Trial: Preliminary Comment." In *Thomas More's Trial by Jury: A Procedural and Legal Review with a Collection of Documents*, edited by Henry Ansgar Kelly, Louis W. Karlin, and Gerard B. Wegemer, 111–19. Woodbridge: Boydell, 2011.

Van Seters, John. *The Edited Bible: The Curious History of the "Editor" in Biblical Criticism*. Winona Lake, IN: Eisenbrauns, 2006.

Vázquez de Prada, Andrés. *Sir Tomás Moro. Lord Canciller de Inglaterra*. 8th ed. Madrid: Rialp, 2004.

Vermeulen, Han F. "Anthropology in Colonial Contexts: The Second Kamchatka Expedition (1733–1743) and the Danish-German Arabia Expedition (1761–

1767)." In *Anthropology and Colonialism in Asia and Oceania*, edited by Jan Van Bremen and Akitoshi Shimizu, 13–39. Richmond, Surrey: Curzon, 1999.

Vermeulen, Hendrik Frederik. "Early History of Ethnography and Ethnology in the German Enlightenment: Anthropological Discourse in Europe and Asia, 1710–1808." PhD diss., Leiden University, 2008.

Vick, Brian. "Greek Origins and Organic Metaphors: Ideals of Cultural Autonomy in Neo-Humanist Germany from Winckelmann to Curtius." *Journal of the History of Ideas* 63.3 (2002) 483–500.

Vlessing, Odette. "The Excommunication of Baruch Spinoza: A Conflict between Jewish and Dutch Law." *Studia Spinozana* 13 (1997) 15–47.

———. "The Jewish Community in Transition: From Acceptance to Emancipation." *Studia Rosenthaliana* 30 (1996) 195–211.

———. "New Light on the Earliest History of the Amsterdam Portuguese Jews." In vol. 3 of *Dutch Jewish History*, edited by Jozeph Michman, 43–75. Assen: Van Gorcum, 1993.

Waldstein, Michael Maria. "*Analogia Verbi*: The Truth of Scripture in Rudolf Bultmann and Raymond Brown." *Letter & Spirit* 6 (2010) 93–140.

———. "The Foundations of Bultmann's Work." *Communio* 2 (1987) 115–45.

Walls, Andrew F. "William Robertson Smith and the Missionary Movement." In *William Robertson Smith: Essays in Reassessment*, edited by William Johnstone, 101–17. Sheffield: Sheffield Academic, 1995.

Walther, Manfred. "Biblische Hermeneutik und historische Erklärung: Lodewijk Meyer und Benediktus de Spinoza über Norm, Methode und Ergebnis wissenschaftlicher Bibelauslegung." *Studia Spinozana* 11 (1995) 227–99.

Wegemer, Gerard B. *Thomas More: A Portrait of Courage*. Princeton: Scepter, 2009.

Weinfeld, Moshe. *Normative and Sectarian Judaism in the Second Temple Period*. New York: T. & T. Clark, 2005.

Whitelam, Keith W. "William Robertson Smith and the So-Called New Histories of Palestine." In *William Robertson Smith: Essays in Reassessment*, edited by William Johnstone, 180–89. Sheffield: Sheffield Academic, 1995.

Wiker, Benjamin. *Moral Darwinism: How We Became Hedonists*. Downers Grove, IL: InterVarsity, 2002.

Williamson, George S. *The Longing for Myth in Germany: Religion and Aesthetic Culture from Romanticism to Nietzsche*. Chicago: University of Chicago Press, 2004.

Withrington, Donald J. "The School in the Free Church Manse at Keig." In *William Robertson Smith: Essays in Reassessment*, edited by William Johnstone, 41–49. Sheffield: Sheffield Academic, 1995.

Woodbridge, John D. "German Responses to the Biblical Critic Richard Simon: From Leibniz to J. S. Semler." In *Historische Kritik und biblischer Kanon in der deutschen Aufklärung*, edited by Henning Graf Reventlow, Walter Sparn, and John Woodbridge, 65–87. Wiesbaden: Harrassowitz, 1988.

———. "Richard Simon le 'père de la critique biblique.'" In *Le Grand Siècle et la Bible*, edited by J. R. Armogathe, 193–206. Paris: Beauschesne, 1989.

———. "Richard Simon's Reaction to Spinoza's Tractatus theologico-politicus." In *Spinoza in der Frühzeit seiner religiösen Wirkung*, edited by Karlfried Gründer and Wilhelm Schmidt-Biggeman, 201–26. Heidelberg: Lanbert Schneider, 1984.

Yamauchi, Edwin. *Composition and Corroboration in Classical and Biblical Studies*. Philadelphia: Presbyterian & Reformed, 1966.

Yovel, Yirmiyahu. *Spinoza and Other Heretics I: The Marrano of Reason*. Princeton: Princeton University Press, 1989.

———. *Spinoza and Other Heretics II: The Adventures of Immanence*. Princeton: Princeton University Press, 1989.

Zac, Sylvain. *Spinoza et l'interprétation de l'Écriture*. Paris: Presses universitaires de France, 1965.

SUBJECT INDEX

AUTHOR INDEX